REMEMBERING
OUR SPIRIT

a spiritual survival guide

THE PRACTICAL SPIRITUALITY SERIES

By David D. Dameron

Volume One
Remembering Our Spirit

To order additional copies of this book, contact:
Xlibris Corporation
1-888-795-4274
www.Xlibris.com
Orders@Xlibris.com
19025

CONTENTS

I dedicate this book to my son,
Ben, and to my daughter, Amanda.
For years I have taught you about the "magic,"
and I write this book with the hope that its message
will be of value to both of you as well as to everyone
who is drawn to read it. I love you both as your spirits
have always been a gentle reminder
of the divine presence in my life.

ACKNOWLEDGMENTS

A creative endeavor like this one is not done alone, and I have been blessed by the talent this project attracted. I am more grateful than I can say for the advice, ideas and inspiration of a number of friends and family.

To my dear wife and soul mate (and yes, for the skeptics of the world, soul mates do exist), Susan, I thank you for your loving presence and support. You inspire me on a daily basis with the quality of your spirit and the depth of the love in your heart.

To my editor, Denise Stallcup, whose professionalism and creative talent helped me find my own voice for this book. I could not have launched this book without you.

To my friend and author, Kevin Zealburg, who was my pioneer when it came to self-publishing. You inspired me to follow in your footsteps, and I very much appreciate your useful advice on which trails I should and should not follow.

To my spiritual teachers (two of many), authors John and Jan Price. Over the years you taught me how to find my own spirit, and most recently shared with me the "do's and don'ts" of successful publishing.

To the many readers who read for me during the creation of this book and who gave me wonderful feedback and the confidence that helped me see this project through:

Mikail Davenport: You are my definition of friendship. Thank you deeply for your love and support all of these years (and not laughing too loud when we skinny-dipped that night on the beach).

Kate Davenport: I have always admired your talent in working with people. I hope this book serves to inspire you in the way you have inspired me.

Reverend Dr. Homer Bain: Growing up, I probably would have continued attending Sunday school if you had been teaching the classes. You are a wonderful spirit.

John Fritz: Thanks for your integrity and the great work you are doing in the corporate jungle.

Mary Frances Weathersby: My dear friend, another one of my spiritual teachers, and a gifted author who taught me to do "my dance" regardless of how other people might think of me.

Horatio and my other friends: You all know who you are. Please know that, even though I cannot see you, your spirits are a constant presence in my life.

Arthur Douët: I feel so thankful to you for doing the cover art for my book. Your work has inspired me for years as I now see what heaven and earth can look like in the form of art.

"When you embark for strange places, don't leave any of yourself safely on shore. Be brave enough to live life creatively. The creative place is where no one else has ever been. You have to leave the city of your comfort and go into the wilderness of your intuition. You can't get there by bus, only by hard work and risk and by not quite knowing what you're doing. What you'll discover will be wonderful. What you'll discover will be yourself."

—Alan Alda

INTRODUCTION

"In this way the structure of the Universe—I mean, of the heavens and the earth and the whole world—was arranged by one harmony through the blending of the most opposite principles."

—Aristotle, On the World (Ancient Greece)

A re you ready to claim your divine inheritance? I cannot answer that question for you, but I can assure you that I am. In fact, my intention is to claim it, each and every day. I'd like to show you how you can choose to do the same.

Whatever you desire—fulfillment, inner peace, happiness, prosperity, perfect health, a rewarding career, or a loving relationship—these are available to you, and have always been accessible to you and to every other living human being. That is your birthright.

You might ask: If my dreams and desires can be so easily realized, why do I feel my life at times is so lacking in some areas? This book was written to answer that question and to suggest a way for your dreams to become your reality.

Remembering Our Spirit is about helping you to recognize the very essence of your nature, and what you can do to make your dreams and desires manifest. This book will show you how to remember who you are, how to recognize the responsibility that comes with that awareness, and how to make use of the power that results. Where you are in the evolvement of your consciousness is reflected by what you are manifesting in your life, and ultimately by the quality of your life. Our life experiences reveal our potential. As your experiences reveal your potential to you, your day-to-day task and challenge becomes recognizing and staying in contact with your essence, your spirit, regardless of what is occurring in your life.

For most of us, the world we live in is very fast paced. Statistics show that Americans are working longer hours, and that our leisure time has decreased significantly. Many of us are experiencing high levels of stress as a result of a number of factors—our accelerated pace, financial concerns, career and family challenges, and world events such as stock market fluctuations and threats of terrorism and war.

In such times, we can allow external forces to cause us to forget who we really are, and allow ourselves to become immersed in fear, worry and anxiety. Then stress becomes a serious problem in our lives, threatening our physical, emotional and spiritual well-being.

If these challenges are familiar to you from your own life, take heart. Stress is generally manageable, and you can decrease the level of stress in your life through the reference you hold in your hands, *Remembering Our Spirit*. This spiritual survival guide serves as a touchstone to help you find your balance, your inner compass, and to help you remember what you already know: Your life has a purpose beyond the external forces that impact it.

Through this book, I hope you will come to see yourself as a divine human being whose life is greater than the external forces that impact you. In the light of such realization, external forces diminish and fall away. Your experience as a human affords you an opportunity daily to bring forth this true identity—your divinity—through the choices you make.

This book can inspire and challenge you. There may be parts of it that don't mesh with Spirit as you define it, as the people on this planet have many names for the Higher Power that helps us all. And there may be parts of this book that you reject, or do not understand or believe. This book is not meant to convince you to believe one way or another, but, instead, to strengthen what you believe, challenge you in those beliefs that do not serve you, and help you grow beyond them by living a life that reflects Spirit. Ultimately, the truth of any personal doctrine or belief system— yours, or mine—is reflected in the quality of life that a person lives. Life is your best teacher. My hope is that this book, and your own life experiences, will show you your path to Spirit, and, through Spirit, to peace and fulfillment.

Remembering Our Spirit will help you explore your own spirituality in a practical way. What do I mean by "spirituality"? I mean the part of each of us that is incorporeal, the part that many beliefs refer to as the "soul," the essence of true being that gives *meaning* to your life. There is a purpose to life—to each individual life, and to life as a whole on this planet. You are an intimate part of a wonderful unfolding that, daily, hourly, is revealing who and what you really are. This book will make you more aware of your own potential, and help you live the highest quality of life. When you live your life in a spiritual way, every activity is done with care and attention. Each chore and responsibility is carried out with joy and purpose.

~ ~ ~ ~ ~ ~ ~ ~ ~ ~

My own journey in coming to write this book is an example of how spirituality speaks to us, shapes our life and helps us grow into joy and a sense of our own purpose. I am a business consultant by trade, and for the past two decades, I have trained thousands of individuals in the area of time management and personal organization. I have conducted numerous teambuilding sessions, as well as personally coached individuals in corporations on both personal and professional related issues. Over the years, I have taught self-improvement workshops and privately consulted with individuals on specific challenges they faced.

My skills as a business consultant were built through personal experience, and also through my ownership of a bookstore in the early 1980s. I sold books and tapes exploring psychology, metaphysics, theology, science and holistic health. I sponsored hundreds of speakers and workshops on various issues around personal growth and self-improvement. I sponsored these speakers and workshops as part of my career as an owner of a bookstore, but in terms of Spirit, I was learning from experts in the field of human potential, and preparing for the next step on my path as a consultant who works to help people improve their quality of life.

So I became a spiritual researcher and explorer, using what I read and learned in my business life and my personal life as well. Through my research, and my own life experiences, I began to expand my belief system. At the same time, I was learning how to bring forth my hidden potential, and how to understand Spirit. My path, even then, was preparing me to write this book.

I was inspired to do such research and develop my belief system as a result of an experience I had in the late 1970s. I have never written about this experience, and only a handful of people know what I am about to share with you. I have been reluctant to share this experience freely, both because it is very important to me and I felt drawn to nurture it in private, and because I felt I might encounter unfair judgment because of it. But I have reached a place in my life that I do not obsess over what people think of me; and I want you to know the impetus behind the creation of this book, and understand its contents. Here is my story.

In 1978, I was working as a school teacher in San Antonio, Texas. I had met an art teacher in the school where I taught, and over time I began to realize she and I shared many interests. She invited me to attend a course called Concept-Therapy in Fort Worth with her. This course was developed by a chiropractor in the 1930s to help people explore their potential. The founder of the Concept-Therapy movement had correlated various theological, scientific and psychological belief systems to provide people with insights and strategies that they could draw on to live a more fulfilling life.

I was interested in what my friend told me, so I drove to Fort Worth for the twenty-three—hour course, taught over one weekend. To be honest, I found the material from the course intriguing, but I didn't understand everything being taught. I drove back to San Antonio and continued with my life as a teacher, glancing at the course material from time to time over the next few months. Then, the following spring, I received a call from the course instructor, and that call was the beginning of a new direction in my life.

The instructor told me there was going to be a week-long training course in Dallas in July for those interested in teaching Concept-Therapy. Being a teacher, and looking for ways to make extra money, I thought the class would be a good way to earn a second income by teaching people this philosophy. I had been drawn to the material from the first, and felt it would be beneficial to me and to others, and thought the week-long course would help me understand the material and the concepts well enough to offer them to others.

So I gladly agreed to take the class, and drove up to Dallas from San Antonio with some friends who were also going to the training. It was a five hour drive, and I remember how excited I was, without really understanding why I was so drawn to the training.

The training was to be held at a Dallas hotel, and when I walked into the meeting room, I remember it was huge. Over two hundred people would be taking this workshop. The room was filled with people setting up for the event. Watching them, I was filled with anticipation, even though I had no idea what was about to happen to me.

That night, before the workshop began, I could not sleep, though I normally sleep easily and deeply. I recall pacing my hotel room. Why was I so excited? What was happening to me? All these questions would soon be answered, but in a way I could never have anticipated.

We arrived at the workshop before nine the next morning, ready to attend for the next five days from 9:00 A.M. to 10:00 P.M. each day, with appropriate breaks. The first two days of the workshop were filled with various teachers instructing us on the background and the basic tenets of Concept-Therapy. I was captivated by the ideas presented, but still found myself struggling to understand everything being taught. Then, on the morning of the third day of the workshop, I experienced something remarkable that I am still unable to fully explain.

A seasoned instructor in Concept-Therapy was speaking to us about the great Hindu text, the *Bhagavad Gita*. I had no idea what the instructor was saying; he might as well have been speaking Russian. But apart from the words I was hearing, suddenly, in a flash, I felt an unbelievable change come over me. The top of my head felt like it was exploding. And in that moment, I went from being unable to understand what the instructor was saying to fully comprehending every word. As understanding washed over me in waves, I began to make connections with the instruction from the previous two days as well. Suddenly and dramatically, all the concepts, ideas and possibilities were falling into place, and I felt an incredible surge of energy.

Inside my head, there was a movie playing. Imagine you are sitting in an auditorium, watching the curtain open to a play that is about to be presented. In my head, a curtain opened, and I saw the purpose of life. I heard voices instructing me, showing me the connections between approaches and theories, and how the machinery of the universe works. All of this happened in a single moment. I became aware that I was having trouble breathing and was beginning to hyperventilate, and I leaned over to my friends sitting next to me and told them I needed their help.

Concerned, my friends took me outside and asked what was going on. I tried to explain, but I had no words to express what I was feeling, seeing and hearing. I was still in the grip of the experience and outside, everything around me seemed alive with energy. I felt everyone and everything was connected by some magical and mystical force. After a few moments, my breathing began to steady, and I felt ready to go back inside; but I was no longer the same person I had been.

The visions continued, all through the afternoon and evening. That night, I began calling some of my friends in San Antonio. I tried to explain to them what was happening to me, but none of them had any frame of reference for my experience, and they didn't seem to know how to relate to me or what to say. I returned to the workshop the next morning, and the final two days of instruction were electrifying. I had an immediate and complete understanding of what each instructor was saying. When the week concluded, my friends and I drove back to San Antonio together, and the five-hour drive seemed like five minutes.

I moved through the next few months in a frenzy of activity. Though I had previously disliked reading, I began reading two or three books each week on spirituality, religion, psychology, metaphysics and science. I felt in contact with a power that continued to guide me; walking into a bookstore, I heard a voice instructing me on buying a particular book. Skills with which I had no previous experience at all began to manifest, as on the day I walked into a store, sat down at a piano and began playing as though I had played all of my life.

I began knowing, instinctively, what people were going to say, and my friends began to joke that I finished everyone's sentences before they could finish them themselves. I was guided to start a bookstore that held the kinds of books I had begun reading, the bookstore that I mentioned at the start of this introduction. There are a number of other stories and occurrences from this time that affirm the great change taking place in my life. Some stories are filled with joy; others are less positive. Not everyone understood what had happened to me. My own parents were extremely concerned about me and thought I had been brainwashed by some cult.

In later years, I was told by some of my spiritual teachers that what I had experienced had been an *illumination*. For whatever reason, I had, in that moment in the workshop, been given certain gifts of knowledge to use in helping others. I would call my illumination an epiphany—a deep realization or insight that occurred in a single moment. To this day, I still do not totally understand what happened to me. I only know that something enormous, something magical, did, indeed, happen.

Though this moment is very much a part of who I am, I have, until now, been reluctant to share this story. It is not my desire to be labeled a mental misfit; I am not a psychic or a New Age channeler. I simply consider myself to be a very ordinary person who had an extraordinary experience. But I felt it important that readers of this book understand its source. It is my belief that the messages imparted to you in this book are divine messages you are meant to be given. If you cannot believe that, or if you cannot relate to my own story, it doesn't matter. What matters are the changes this book can bring to your own life. So, in a sense, I am, after all, a channel of the Divine. But so are you, as you will discover.

You may not hear voices or see visions, but each living being has his or her own unique gifts and approaches in our relationship with the Divine Force, with Spirit. The challenge for all of us is to become more aware of our divine nature, establish a connection with it and maintain that connection.

You are your own ultimate authority. I can only share with you what I have learned from personal experience. These are my truths; I believe they are also universal truths, and of use to you. But I always remind my clients to question authority, and to disbelieve anything they have not tested for validity. It is enough that you read this book, think about its passages and let the experiences of your life serve as your guide for your own truths.

～ ～ ～ ～ ～ ～ ～ ～ ～

The areas I have chosen to share with you in this book evolved, in part, from the questions I have been asked by my clients over the years as they struggled with various aspects of their lives, or as they tried to understand why certain things in their lives had happened. After years of consulting and working with people, I began to see their questions had a familiar pattern to them, springing from sources that are the subjects of this book. Here are some of the questions I heard most frequently:

- Is there a Higher Power, and if so, how can I come to understand how it operates?
- How do I become more aware and evolve my consciousness?
- Is there a purpose to life?
- How does attitude impact one's life, and how can I change my mental outlook?
- How do the choices I make impact my life, and how do I stop making poor choices?
- How do I appreciate more the abundance life has offered me and others?
- How can I find the courage to make the changes I know I need to make in my life?

- I sometimes lose faith that my life can be turned around. How can I strengthen my faith?
- I know I should be grateful for what I have in life, but I tend to concentrate more on what I don't have instead of what I do have. How do I embrace gratitude?
- What is love? How can I love myself more in the best way? How can I be better able to express love more?

~ ~ ~ ~ ~ ~ ~ ~ ~

These questions are indicative of the crisis I see in those I counsel, in our nation and in life in the modern world. They are eternal questions, asked by people in every century. But they are questions that require thought, and the fast pace of our lives, and its emphasis on the material, put us at a disadvantage in seeking answers to them. The problems of our day and age—long work hours, careers that are less than fulfilling, relationships that fall apart, and health issues related to stress—are only symptoms of a much greater problem. I see the real challenge of our day as being a crisis in spirit.

What do I mean by a crisis in spirit? Many of the individuals I coach are not in touch with their potential. They do not understand *the power of choice*—that they can help create the world they desire by making more empowered choices. When someone says to me that they refuse to consider making changes in their habits, because they have lived that way all their life, that is a crisis in spirit. When someone feels stuck in his or her career, and feel they are too old to make a change, or feel their talents are unmarketable—that is a crisis in spirit. It is the same with other changes people tell me they would like to make, but feel are impossible—the single parent who says she is working two jobs while raising her children, and who has no hope that things can get better. My single friends who tell me they have given up on finding Mr. or Ms. Right—all of these are crises in spirit.

This book is to help you get in touch with your own spirit, and to help you make choices and take appropriate actions to bring to you *the most important things your heart desires*. Take this book with you wherever you go. Open it up to any section, read the passage, reflect on it for a few minutes, and consciously reconnect, in those moments, with your own divinity. In doing so, you'll be sending your thoughts, feelings and intentions out to the Universe, and the Universe will return them to you in physical form. What does your heart desire? A new career, health, financial abundance, a soul mate, or anything you long for, as well as the grace to be serene in adversity—all can magically appear in response to this process. When you are experiencing a crisis or challenge, keep reading this book, and *remember* to stay in connection with your divinity. Soon, the crisis will disappear, leaving behind valuable lessons that will take you further on the path to your destiny.

~ ~ ~ ~ ~ ~ ~ ~ ~

How to Use This Book

Each chapter in this book starts with a short story and commentary to give you a foundation in the ten concepts that will put you in touch with Spirit. The story and commentary are followed by brief thoughts, stories, examples of the chapter's subject at work. Each brief passage is on its own page to leave room for the most important writing in this book—your own thoughts, ideas and insights. Below each brief passage is a section inviting you to record your own thoughts.

I suggest that you do not read this book quickly, but that you stop and reflect on each story and each passage. The gift of each passage may not reveal itself to you immediately, and reading slowly gives your own spirit time to connect with the material, and with you. Likewise, a passage may not reveal itself to you the first time you read it. Some of the passages will resonate after you have connected with other passages, so feel free to open a part of the book you've read at random, and read the passages again.

This is an ongoing process. I recommend you carry this book with you so you can jot down insights or experiences that resonate with the passages in the book. Spirit will respond to the work you do, and the insights and experiences it offers will become your own personal daily reminders of your divine nature.

Once again, *please take time to meditate on these passages.* Though they are short, there is great depth to them. When the sculptor, Michelangelo, was asked what he envisioned in a block of marble he was about to carve, he replied that he saw an angel, and that he was trying to free her from the stone. You are that stone, and the spirit inside you is waiting to be freed.

It is my sincere wish for you to be empowered to live the highest quality of life that you desire and deserve. If this book can assist you in this journey, my heart is filled with joy for you. The most important moment in our lives is the moment in which we choose love over fear. Remember that we have the opportunity to make each day—starting with this very day—special, by connecting with this spirit. This day, I will remember!

CHAPTER 1

SPIRIT

" . . . and know each other as one deity. The Spirit shall look out through Matter's gaze and Matter shall reveal the Spirit's face. Then man and superman shall be at one and all the earth become a single life."

—Aurobindo, from Savitri (Hinduism)

Betty, a close professional colleague of mine, was recently conducting a teambuilding workshop for one of her clients at a ranch just north of San Antonio. She was working with the participants on what is called a "Ropes Course." On a Ropes Course there are various balance beams and obstacles designed to challenge the participants' abilities and test their skills in communication and cooperation.

The final test of the ropes course is called the "Zip Line." Participants are asked to climb a pole to a platform that is about one hundred feet in the air. Each individual is strapped into a harness that is attached to a line stretching fifty yards over a canyon. Attached to the harness, each participant is pushed from the platform and rides through the canyon to a telephone pole on the other side. Once on the other side, the participant must balance and climb down the pole.

Betty was the last to ride the zip line, and, to her surprise and embarrassment, as she climbed the pole she began crying. Her body shook. From the platform, she looked out over the precipice and knew, in her heart, that if she left the platform she would fall from the zip line. She began saying, again and again, "I can't do this." Her clients responded by encouraging her to keep climbing, but Betty realized her fear of heights was overwhelming her in this situation. She was terrified, and was also embarrassed to be breaking down emotionally in front of her clients.

After some coaxing from the zip line instructor, Betty made up her mind to jump in spite of her fears. She held onto the harness with all of her might as she was pushed across the canyon. As she opened her eyes, she noticed that her hands were turning white from holding on so hard. In that instant she realized that she was attached to a harness which was connected to a thick metal wire. Her grip on the line was of no use; it was an exercise in futility, and was not an element of the situation at all.

"Why am I holding on so hard?" Betty mumbled to herself. The harness was holding her safe. So she let go of the harness. Upon landing at the end of the zip line, she climbed down the pole, sobbing the whole time. But her tears were not out of fear or anxiety. They were tears of joy. The exercise had taught her how much she had been holding on all her life. She had always felt alone and risks were hard for her to take. She realized that she lacked trust in her spiritual life as well. She had not trusted Spirit to support her, just as she had not trusted the harness to support her. Betty had always believed until this day that she alone had to make everything happen in her life. As a result of her experience with the harness, and with trust, she decided not to hold on anymore in her life, but to take the leap and take risks.

~ ~ ~ ~ ~ ~ ~ ~ ~

This chapter is about Spirit. It is about your divinity and the realization that there is no separation between yourself and Spirit other than what you perceive and create. Imagine, in your mind's eye, a circle on a piece of paper. This circle represents everything that exists in the Universe—all galaxies, all planets—everything. Nothing exists outside of the circle. What you are looking at is the totality of God.

This divine force is everywhere (omnipresent), all-knowing (omniscient), and all-powerful (omnipotent). If everything in the circle is representative of this divine force, then where are you? The answer is that you live in the circle, and *you literally live in God.* You are an aspect of this divine force. You, too, are everywhere, connected to all of life, all-knowing and all-powerful. And everyone on this planet is an aspect of the Divine, just as you are.

Only one thing keeps you from truly understanding your divine heritage: your lack of awareness that you are a divine being. In the Bible, Jesus spoke many times implying that we are divine beings. He urged us to realize that we could be more than a human being by being as he was. To know Jesus was to know our father. To know ourselves is to know our divinity.

Conventional opinion and theological doctrine often do not support the viewpoint that we are divine beings. Most theological doctrines tend to emphasize separation. Whether you believe in a higher power or whether you see yourself only as a human being does not diminish how Spirit operates. It is impersonal. You have been given the free will to create the type of life you choose. God just meets us where we are in our awareness.

Finally, when we were given the power of choice—to choose the world we desire—it was as if Spirit gave up its life for us. This is like someone dying who leaves an inheritance for his or her loved ones. If Spirit is perfection then what was left in its inheritance for us is perfection! We only need to claim it by our thoughts, feelings, and actions.

Imagine what your life could be if your every thought, word and action came from your conception of yourself as Spirit. Peace, harmony, abundance, love and fulfillment would be your divine inheritance, and that inheritance waits at your fingertips, yours to claim. The choice is yours. The kingdom of heaven is at hand.

~ ~ ~ ~ ~ ~ ~ ~ ~

This book is interactive; it suggests that you journal your own responses, thoughts and inspirations. The following reflections and experiences are my own. I hope they will lead you to your own insights, and to record those insights in the space at the bottom of each page. Please take your time with these exercises, as that will give the divine voice inside you a chance to grow and make itself heard.

I misplaced my car keys today, and became extremely exasperated searching for them. I finally sat down, closed my eyes, and asked Spirit to show me where they were. After doing some chores, a picture appeared in my mind of the bench outside of our front door. I went to look there and, sure enough, found my car keys. I want to remember to ask for guidance from the Divine, in matters large and small. I know I will always receive an answer if I am patient and willing to listen.

My Thoughts—

"Ask and it will be given you; knock, and the door will be opened to you."

—Matthew 7:7

To me, the greatest act of love is the gift God gave when He said "I give you me." This divine power said "I will let you create the life you choose. I will grant whatever you ask me to do. I will assist you when you need help. I will guide you when you need direction. I will let you create your world in any way you choose. I am with you always in your moments of joy and in the depths of your darkness." Oh, how I desire to bring Spirit into my heart in each moment to embrace this reality of life, to know that I am never alone and that the all-powerful Divine Force supports me.

My Thoughts—

"If God made us in His image, we have certainly returned the compliment."

—Voltaire

I want to claim my inheritance as a divine being. I want to learn how this divine power operates and learn how to stay in connection with it. I start by recognizing when this power is at work in my life. I ask myself: What do I feel when I am connection with the Divine Power? I feel joy, excitement, peace, love, harmony, and compassion. These feelings are quite different from the way I feel when I am not in connection with the Divine. Then I feel depressed, anxious or upset. How can I discover how God operates, connect with this awesome force and remain in connection with it?

My Thoughts—

"When you search for me, you will find me."

—Jeremiah

I was taking a workshop and, during the instruction, was often distracted by a decision I was facing. I was trying to decide whether I should spend $1800 on a new piece of office equipment. At the break, I went to my hotel room for a few moments and was switching through some channels on the television set. I came to the weather channel station; this particular station normally has affirmations and suggestions that scroll past at the bottom of the television screen. But today only one scroll appeared at the bottom of the screen. There, scrolling below the day's weather, was the message: "Get your head and heart going in the right direction and you will not be disappointed." On the following day, I received a check for $1800 in the mail, sent by a family member who had been handling a family matter for me. Spirit works in wondrous ways.

My Thoughts—

"Make me do what I already know."

—Emerson

When I am speaking of my interpretation of the Divine, I must remember to be respectful of others and of all religious traditions and spiritual beliefs. I now know that it makes no difference what name we give to the Divine. Whether we refer to the Divine as God, the Great Spirit, Brahman, Deity, Yahweh or by any other name, I know I and others are dealing with only one source which manifests in many ways.

My Thoughts—

"It is a mistake to assume that God is interested only, or even chiefly, in religion."

—William Temple, British Archbishop

I went to work today and made a decision that I would treat everyone as if they were Spirit (which they are!). And as a result, I had a great day. I found I was more open to different people's personalities and diversities. Traffic did not bother me. My dogs responded to my loving touch. My wife said I looked happy. My challenge is to be able to hold these thoughts and feelings of Deity all of the time. Today, I really learned how life is a mirror—a reflection of my thoughts and feelings. What I project is what looks back at me.

My Thoughts—

"The eye with which I see God is the same as that which sees me."

—Meister Eckhart

My wife and I were struggling to decide whether or not to proceed with remodeling our house. It was a major financial decision for us. The money we needed to complete the job had not come to us yet. We each finally decided to meditate on our dilemma and ask Spirit. When we came back to compare notes, both of our inner voices had asked us essentially the same question: "What do you want?" We decided to do the remodeling. The money for the project appeared two weeks later. What I learned from this experience is that what I truly desire will always be granted and has always been available to me if I can see, feel, and be willing to act on whatever I desire.

My Thoughts—

"I will instruct you and search you the way you should go."

—Psalm 51:12

When I am feeling stuck or unsure about something, I ask my inner guide what is preventing my heart's desires from manifesting. I know that God holds nothing back from me. Whatever I ask and whatever I need are given to me freely by Spirit. My part is only to ask for what I want with great feeling. Feeling—connection—is the magnet that attracts whatever thing or answer I desire in life. And once I ask, I must pay attention and listen. How does Spirit communicate with me?

My Thoughts—

"Everything in life is speaking in spite of its apparent silence."

—Hazrat Inayet Khan

Heaven on earth will manifest for me when I totally embrace my divinity. I cannot make a choice to harm someone or break a law if I am truly living my life from Spirit. I best serve others in my life, and thus myself, when I make divine choices. I am a better father, a more loving husband, a trusted friend, and a more influential teacher when I am embracing life from my spirit. In what ways am I already doing a good job of connecting with my spirit? And how can I use those connections to show me how to embrace my divinity even more?

My Thoughts—

"We are not separate from being, we are in it."

—Plotinus

I ask myself that if I am an aspect of God, then who is there to turn to with my problems? I know God is not in the sky or a force outside myself. I realize that the Divine is everywhere. The answer to my question is in the question. There is a part of me which is divine and a piece of me that is human. I am learning how to merge the two, much like bringing heaven (my divinity) and earth (my humanity) together. I choose to turn my desires and questions over to my divine self. What things have I been able to turn over to God in this way? How can I use those experiences to help me access the divine voice within me?

My Thoughts—

"I know I am God because when I pray to him I find I'm talking to myself."

—Peter Barnes, British playwright

Today, I experienced many problems and a great deal of frustration. My computer was freezing up on me. A number of clients called to reschedule classes. Traffic was horrible. The grocery store was a nightmare. I felt uptight and irritated. And the more stressed I became, the more things seemed to go wrong. It is in these moments that I know I am out of connection with my inner spirit. It helps me to recognize these feelings, step back and say: Where is my divinity in these moments? How can I access the Divine within me to break this cycle?

My Thoughts—

"God is subtle, but he is not malicious."

—Albert Einstein

Here is my list that reminds me of things that help me stay in connection with Spirit:

1. Play my favorite music.
2. Read from an inspirational book.
3. Rent one of my favorite movies.
4. Work in the garden.
5. Play with my dogs.
6. Take a bubble bath with my wife.
7. Call my kids.
8. Schedule a massage.
9. Open a door for someone.
10. Meditate.
11. Take a nap.
12. Laugh.
13. Cry.

What things help you stay in connection with Spirit?

My Thoughts—

"Whatever you attempt, go at it with Spirit."

—David Starr Jordan

I must admit there are times I ask the question: "Do I really believe I am an aspect of God?" It is in these moments that I reaffirm: "I have come to this lifetime to represent my divinity. I totally accept my divinity and all that I desire in life. Thank you, God, for my most fabulous life." In thanking God, I am giving thanks to myself. When I look in the mirror, I am looking at God. What an awesome feeling and responsibility, and what a gift.

My Thoughts—

"For everything that lives is holy."

—William Blake

Everything in my life is in divine right order, and I now recognize, accept and follow the divine plan of my life as it reveals itself to me. In every decision I need to make, I ask my higher self—my divinity—what I should do in this moment? I am learning how to recognize what the message from Spirit feels like.

My Thoughts—

"I am with you always."

—Matthew 28:20

CHAPTER 2

CONSCIOUSNESS

"I say that all are calling on the same God . . . It is not good
to feel that my religion is true and other religions are false.
All seek the same object."

—Ramakrisna (Hinduism)

One of the most endearing stories that I have ever heard is "The Rabbi's Gift." Although I have been told many versions of this well-known tale, I thought it would be appropriate in our discussion on the subject of consciousness to tell it again in my own words.

Once there was an old monastery that was slowly deteriorating into ruin. There were only seven brothers left to take care of it. The gardens outside had died long ago, and the children and the families from the village no longer came to the monastery grounds to play and have picnics.

Inside the structure the picture was even more grim. The food was running out, and there was no money to buy supplies. One night the brothers called a meeting to discuss their plight.

They gathered around a circular table in the Great Hall. Each of them spoke in turn, and it was apparent that their hearts were filled with sadness. Each of them shared stories of the days when the monastery had been alive and vibrant. As they spoke of their fond memories, it was obvious that each was sharing in the responsibility for the demise of the sanctuary.

One of the brothers said, "We need advice and we need it immediately." Another responded, "Why has God abandoned us in our need?" Soon everyone was arguing and pointing fingers at each other in blame. Finally, the elder of the group stood and tapped his cane on the floor. Everyone respected Brother Thomas' opinions and insights so they stopped bickering and listened.

Brother Thomas spoke in a peaceful tone. "There is someone

who can help us. His wisdom has been known to us for years. Although his religious beliefs and customs are different than ours, he has always possessed divine insight. I am saying to each of you that I believe that the rabbi has the answer for us."

The brothers looked at one another. They had forgotten about the rabbi who traveled once a year to their village and stayed in a small hut on the other side of the hill. They also realized, as Brother Thomas had, that the rabbi was visiting the village at this time.

Brother Thomas suggested that one of the brothers travel across the valley and over the mountain to visit the rabbi. Since Brother Thomas was too old and weak to make the journey, it was agreed that Brother Benjamin should make the trip, and he agreed with great enthusiasm.

The next morning was cloudy. Brother Benjamin packed up some supplies, said goodbye to everyone and began his trek to the rabbi's hut. During the journey, his thoughts were on the brothers and the monastery. He knew his trip must be successful, or all would be lost. After several hours, he arrived at the hut where the rabbi lived, and he knocked on the door.

The rabbi opened the door and, recognizing Brother Benjamin, embraced him. The two men sat down at the kitchen table and Brother Benjamin told of the sad plight of the monastery and his brothers. The rabbi listened intently. After hearing the entire story, the rabbi stood up, paced back and forth, and delivered this message to Brother Benjamin.

"My friend, I am deeply moved by your plight, and if it was within my power, I would do anything I could do to help you. But I must say that what you have told me is not unique; I am hearing in every village I travel. It appears that people have lost hope, and their faith is being tested by what *appears* to be insurmountable challenges. I will tell you what I told them. I do not have the answer for you, but I will say one thing that you can tell to your group. *One of you is the Christ!*"

Stunned, Brother Benjamin rose from his chair to thank the rabbi and left the hut to finish the journey that he had started that morning. He was perplexed by what the rabbi had said. How could one of them be the Christ? That night, he arrived back at the monastery, and the brothers greeted him at the door with great fervor. They sat at the table and listened intently to his tale.

Brother Benjamin looked at everyone at the table and told them what the rabbi had said; that "one of us is the Christ!" Brother Timothy rose from the table defiantly. "That is blasphemous," he said. Brother Victor interrupted and remarked though that the rabbi was a very wise man. "When can any of you ever remember the rabbi being wrong?" he asked.

But the brothers could reach no agreement. The meeting broke up, and Brother Thomas instructed everyone to reflect upon the rabbi's words. "We will meet again tomorrow morning," he said, and each brother went back to his room to contemplate what the rabbi had said.

In their rooms, the brothers thought about each other and tried to envision each of their brothers as the Christ. Their thoughts went like this: "How could Brother Thomas be the Christ? He is old and crotchety; but it's true, he always did possess that innate wisdom. And Brother Victor is always yelling about something, but even so, his will and motivation have always been an inspiration considering that he had many health problems."

So it was that, as each brother thought about the other, they came up with reasons why each person might and might not be the Christ. Each brother had a unique and challenging personality. But when each brother contemplated his fellow brothers, he found that there were definite Christ-like qualities about each one, and definite qualities that were not at all Christ-like. When they met again next morning, they realized sadly that they still had no answer and the question remained: Who was the Christ?

Months later, the rabbi decided to visit the monastery. He crested the top of the last hill and what he saw brought tears to his eyes. The monastery grounds were filled with children playing and families enjoying themselves. The gardens were luscious and immaculate and filled with every conceivable flower and vegetable. Even the walls of the monastery seemed to glisten in the sun.

The rabbi joined the brothers for a meal, and when they had

eaten, he asked, "What happened? How did this change manifest?" This is what he learned.

Following their night of contemplation, each brother kept wondering who was truly the Christ. On the off chance that one of them was truly the Christ, they started treating each other better and with a sense of reverence. And even more importantly, each of the brothers began treating himself better, too, on the off chance that he himself was, without knowing it, the Christ.

~ ~ ~ ~ ~ ~ ~ ~ ~

In treating each other and themselves from the perspective that they were the Christ, the brothers created a place of love, gratitude and reverence that began to be reflected in their outer surroundings. But the change really took place first inside themselves—in their *consciousness!*

How you perceive your outer environment, and how you shape it, is totally influenced by your state of consciousness. *Roget's Super Thesaurus* defines consciousness as "the power of being conscious; sensation, awareness, cognizance, recognition, mindfulness." When you become more aware that you truly are a divine being, then you make your choices from that awareness; and then all things become possible.

In the age of Socrates, Plato, and Aristotle, two words were identified as being the keys to divine enlightenment: *Know thyself.* These two words were the key for an individual to evolve spiritually.

According to Reuters News Service, a recent Johns Hopkins study presented May 10, 2002, at the American Geriatrics Society's annual meeting found that people who are more spiritual are better able to deal with the discomforts of life. Even more important, though, was the definition the Hopkins researchers gave spirituality: "The capacity of an individual to stand outside of his or her immediate sense of time and space and to view life from a larger, more detached perspective."

From that detached perspective, you realize that every experience you attract to yourself is helping you to become more aware of your divinity.

Unfortunately, our society has not put a high value on self-awareness, and that prevents many people from being consciously aware of their divine potential. We tend to evaluate our lives based on what we attain in the non-spiritual realms: jobs, money, relationships, material things. We fail to realize that consciousness comes first, that we, in our divinity, are the *cause* of how things manifest. Always remember that to truly know yourself is to know your divinity as the source of where things manifest in your own life and in the phenomenal world in which we live!

I learned a new technique today to put a stop to any negative thoughts which I may be having and any negative words I utter. I just need to say one word, twice: *cancel, cancel.* I know that my words and thoughts create what I attract to myself. Do I want to attract positive things in my life, or do I want to create negative things? I am more aware in each moment of what I think and what I say.

My Thoughts—

.

"We sit together, the mountain and I, until only the mountain remains."

—Li Po

If God is everywhere, all-knowing, and all-powerful, then there can be no lack. Anything I need has already been given, even if it is not yet visible to my eyes. But if I see below the surface and realize that what I need is ready to come into manifestation, then my only avenue is to seek connection with my divinity to bring it into form. Spirit is who I am and is the source of the manifestation of my desires.

My Thoughts—

"For we see what he has made us . . . which God prepared beforehand to be our way of life."

—Ephesians 2:10

When I become conscious of the dream I want, then Spirit can manifest my desire. I have to believe it. I have to feel it. There was a time that the only dream my consciousness could embrace was the dream of a four figure income a year. Now that I am making a six figure income, my awareness has expanded; I know my consciousness can do far more than I can ever conceive to ask of it. Spirit fills our desires to the size of the awareness we impress on it. Is anything keeping me from further expanding my consciousness in any aspect of my life?

My Thoughts—

"Man's desires are limited by his perceptions; none can desire what he has not perceived."

—William Blake

I attract situations in my life which at times test my resolve and demonstrate where I am in my consciousness. I welcome these gifts as my teachers and a barometer of where I am in my awareness. Any situation which causes a major emotional reaction inside me is an opportunity for me to heal something inside myself. What things do I allow to cause a negative reaction on my part? What lesson is my consciousness trying to teach me, and what can I learn from them?

My Thoughts—

"I saw it, but I did not realize it."

—Elizabeth Peabody, US Educator

I am having difficulty with one of my clients. I feel very reactive over his leadership style and his unwillingness to listen to my guidance. I feel myself wanting to avoid him, and am very upset about this. But it is useful to ask: What is this client showing me about myself that is causing this strong internal reaction? What other people have caused these reactions in me? I know that such people have become my best teachers.

My Thoughts—

"Only that day dawns to which we are awake."

—Henry David Thoreau

One of the basic tenets in solving a problem is to deal with it from the source, from where the problem began. In the business world, this is called Root Cause Analysis. I now realize that when I see all things happening in my life, good or bad, from a spiritual viewpoint, then I can truly heal things inside myself. I have found that fear is the root cause of most of my problems. I am developing my awareness to understand that nothing happens by chance. Every day is an opportunity for growth. I am not afraid.

My Thoughts—

"When you really look for me, you will see me instantly—
you will find me in the tiniest house of time."

—Kabir

The wisdom of God is flowing through me now. The pushing I feel from within at times is Spirit telling me to move in a new direction. With my new eyes I see beyond the outer form of things to their essence. I see the divinity in everything that is coming into form. By doing this, I am tapping into how things really manifest in my life. God is my source. I am my source when I approach life from my divinity.

My Thoughts—

"The true value of a human being is determined primarily by the measure and sense in which he has attained liberation from the self."

—Albert Einstein

When I observe the various forms of life on this planet, the marvelous ways our bodies function, an ecosystem which was perfectly created to maintain life on this planet, and the many miracles which have happened in my life and in others, I am constantly reminded of a divine force in operation. Each day I see the Divine at work in all people and in all situations that I encounter.

My Thoughts—

"No man is an island, entire of itself; every man is a piece of the continent, a part of the main . . ."

—John Donne

As a divine being, I am like a radio station sending out information as well as receiving impulses. If I can learn to adjust the dials in my consciousness so my transmissions and the messages I receive have no static, then I can tune my inner station into the divine channel which can have unbelievable effects on my life. What does the divine impulse feel like to me?

My Thoughts—

"What your attention is upon, you become."

—Pearl Dorris

My wife always finds the best-tasting watermelons when she goes to the grocery store. I seem to bring home ones which are less than ripe. I asked her one day how she selects melons. She said she just asks Spirit which one she should pick, and she responds by picking up which melon *feels* right. This may seem like a small thing; but Spirit does not judge our dreams or desires. It only wants to help us realize them. My scientific approach of thumping the melon or looking for a brown stem is not working very well for me. I need to remind myself to keep asking Spirit for guidance. If Spirit will guide us in choosing our food, in what greater ways can I make use of this divine gift? In what other situations, large or small, could I utilize Spirit's help?

My Thoughts—

"Knowledge speaks, but wisdom listens."

—Oliver Wendall Holmes

Without a doubt, I feel the presence of Spirit when I am around babies. My wife and I were visiting with our niece, who recently gave birth to a beautiful baby girl. When I looked into her eyes and felt her touch, I knew I was in the presence of Spirit. I recalled the time when my two children were born how I had felt similar feelings in their new presences. I also needed to remind myself when they became teenagers that they were still spiritual beings! Who else have I forgotten is part of Spirit?

My Thoughts—

"What you are looking for is who is looking."

—Saint Francis

Death is not the final stage in our evolution. That message came to me during my own illumination, and the message was recently confirmed in the transitions of my parents. I feel that they are around me and letting me know that they are okay. Having that awareness that they are always near me helps me to deal with missing the physical presence of loved ones when they pass on. One of their messages to me is to never take life for granted. Live each day to the fullest. Live each moment in connection with my divinity.

My Thoughts—

"We know what we are, but know not what we may be."

—William Shakespeare

I realized today that there will not be peace on earth until the majority of the world's population embraces the concept that we are all from one source. If we remain conscious that everyone is part of the divine essence, and operates from that source, we cannot bring ourselves to hurt others. Likewise, Spirit helps me prioritize. I cannot worry about money or power when I am living from Spirit. I promote peace on earth in each moment that I am aware of my divinity and the divinity of those around me. What did I do today to deepen that realization?

My Thoughts—

"Conscience is the inner voice that warns us somebody may be looking."

—H L Mencken

My wife and I engaged the services of a pet psychic that many of our friends had used. Our friends spoke highly of her, and we thought, at the very least, it would be entertaining to have her come and tell us what our dogs were thinking. After a session with this lady, we were convinced that animals have spirits and are aware of much more than we ever had thought. She told us things that only we (and our dogs) could know. As a result, I gave a great deal of thought to the consciousness of all living beings. I now have a deeper connection with our dogs and with all animals in general. Just as we do not want to bring harm to human beings who are really divine beings, I have a new respect for the consciousness of animals (who are also of Spirit), and I feel animal abuse should never be tolerated!

My Thoughts—

"Love me, love my dog."

—Proverb

I am told that there is a spectacular grove of aspen trees in Colorado. On the surface, the trees appear to be solitary, of different sizes and in different locations. But under the earth's surface, these trees are part of one great root system. This marvel of nature reminds me that on this planet, we appear to be many races and genders. But in reality, we are connected to one source.

My Thoughts—

"The real voyage of discovery consists not in seeking new lands but seeing with new eyes."

—Marcel Proust

When I was expanding my consulting and training business many years ago, I would be asked to speak at conferences or similar types of gatherings. When I saw some of the speakers invited to these events, I would become insecure since I was not as well-known as they were. Today, my consciousness and confidence no longer compares myself to others. I have some wonderful messages as they do to share with my audiences.

My Thoughts—

"Each person's work is always a portrait of himself."

—Samuel Butler

Many years ago, I would have looked at working in the yard—mowing, weeding, and planting—as a chore and resist doing these things. Today, I approach my yard work with joy as I now see this work as an expression of Spirit. What I plant and tend to soon becomes beautiful flowers, trees, or vegetables. I have become aware of Spirit more as I work in the yard and realize that creating a place of beauty is an expression of Spirit—and my divinity! In what other areas of my life has my consciousness expanded in this way?

My Thoughts—

"Opportunity is missed by most people because it's dressed in overalls and looks like work."

—Thomas Edison

CHAPTER 3

PURPOSE

"I was a hidden treasure and I wanted to be known. That is why I created the world."

—Prophetic Sayings (Hadiths) (Islam)

In 1974, I started teaching with a local school district in San Antonio, Texas. Teaching has always been my first joy. I loved my students very much, and I tried to make my classes fun and informative. Four years into my teaching career, I came across a very special student whose gift to me still touches my heart today.

Jason came to my class as a transfer student in the middle of the school year. He was Chinese-American and, as a result of his parents' jobs, had lived in several locations around the world.

He was a bright boy, responsive to many of our class discussion questions. He was extremely polite and had a great sense of humor which endeared him to everyone in the class. But in spite of his intelligence and enthusiasm, we encountered a problem I had not expected.

I gave Jason and the rest of the class a written exam, and Jason failed it. I was quite surprised; he had done well at answering oral questions in class. I asked him to stay after class to try to understand what had happened on the exam. With tears in his eyes, he told me that he could not read English.

Jason had been someone who had been passed on through our school system without anyone noticing his lack of reading comprehension skills. I told Jason that I would help him, and I began by taking him to the counselor and explaining to her what I had uncovered.

The counselor tested Jason and determined that he had very specific reading and writing problems. She immediately set up tutorial help for him, and for the next two years, he was given extra help to correct his deficiencies. I thought about Jason often over the next two years, always remembering how much I liked him and how much I appreciated the effort that he made for me in class. I never gave much thought to my discovery of his deficiency or what I had done in response.

What I did not know was that Jason's life changed radically as a result of my realization and the actions I took. Jason's reaction to our encounter, he told me later, was that someone cared and understood, and was willing to help him get past something he had held as a deep secret since he had come to this country.

Jason was my student in 1978. For the next fifteen years, I heard from Jason at least once each year, usually around Christmas. He would call me from wherever he was in the world. He telephoned me each year as he went through high school and until he graduated. He continued to contact me when he was in college, and when he went into the military.

As time went on, Jason's communications kept me up with the changes in his life, his marriage and the various changes in his career. Each time this young man called me on the telephone he would tell me how much what I did for him meant to him and how much it had changed his life. He was no longer afraid of being able to communicate. He was able to fit into our society and felt he was given an equal chance to be successful.

Jason felt I had given him a gift, but the gift he gave to me in return was equally great. He shared his heart with me, and his story has given my life *purpose*. I have not heard from Jason in the last few years; but I think of him and his story often. I am always touched by his story because what I did to help him seemed so inconsequential to me at the time. I saw it as just a part of my job, and as something that took no great effort on my part. But, to Jason, my realization and the actions I took were an extraordinary event in his life.

～ ～ ～ ～ ～ ～ ～ ～ ～

Jason's story has made me appreciate the opportunity I have as a teacher, trainer and consultant. Because of him, I know that I have the ability to make a difference in people's lives in a positive way. I also know what I do makes ripples I can never even know; I cannot know how many people I enabled Jason to influence in a positive way because he has skills that give him a place in our society.

You can never know what a simple act of kindness can do for a person. Imagine what our world would be like if everyone awakened each day to try to make a difference in one person's life. What an inspiring and effective life purpose that would give every living human being.

To meet your daily challenges and to evolve spiritually, you need a purpose. Purpose fuels your intentions. Purpose can motivate you and give you goals to strive for. Purpose can provide you with determination, resolve, tenacity, and single-mindedness.

Purpose is part of attracting your divine inheritance. Remember that everything you could possibly desire or need has already been provided for you. By finding meaning in how you conduct your life you create the catalyst for attracting the gifts of your divine inheritance: prosperity, health, fulfilling relationships and self-worth.

In 1969, I was in a car accident with three of my friends as we were going to football practice. The front and back end of my friend's Mustang was totally demolished. The only part of the car which was not damaged was the compartment where the four of us were seated. We, and the police, were all astonished that we had not been injured or killed. I believe that Spirit protected us that day because it had a purpose for each of us. I was allowed to live for a reason, and so were my friends!

My Thoughts—

"I believe we are here for a reason. I believe that as each day unfolds, we see less of the shadow and more of the sun, less of the tarnish and more of the gold."

—C. Hawkinson

The events in your life are a road map. They draw a path that helps you to recognize the signs of the Divine operating in your life. These signs could be in a car in front of you traveling forty miles an hour in a sixty mile per hour zone. They could manifest through the words of song on the radio. You might be sitting outside when a dragonfly lands near you. Did you know that dragonflies are symbolic of something? I must remind myself that everything happening to me has a purpose! Spirit is constantly sending me messages, and I want to develop the ability to hear them.

My Thoughts—

"Living the spiritual life is not only recognizing the Divine Presence in ourselves—but in everyone."

—John Randolph Price

Everything that occurs in your life occurs for the purpose of drawing you closer to your divinity. Every choice you make brings a corresponding result. This is spiritual law. If I am making choices which are out of connection with my spirit, then I will attract events which will try to put me back on course. These events manifest to help me to become more conscious; if I ignore them, I continue to create pain for myself. Everything has meaning.

My Thoughts—

"To everything, there is a season and a time to every purpose under the heaven."

—Ecclesiastes 3:1

There are no ordinary events in your life. Everything you experience is important and is intimately connected to your unfolding story and your divine purpose. I was ready to leave to teach a workshop today when I realized that I had forgotten something. I ran back into the house, and in those few seconds before I returned outside the telephone rang. It was a friend who was in a desperate need. He would not have been able to get hold of me immediately if I had not gone back into my home. Through what other events has Spirit shaped what I did, and the opportunities I realized as a result?

My Thoughts—

"Every living creature coming into the world has something allotted to him to perform, therefore he should not stand an idle spectator of what others are doing."

—Sarah Kirby Trimmer

All things created begin with an idea. As I look around me, I cannot see a single thing that was not originally an idea. I see the majesty in which we live. Where do my ideas come from? From what source can I draw inspiration? Does the miracle you are a part of not suggest that there is a wisdom of something that far surpasses your human understanding? How can we draw upon that power and that wisdom?

My Thoughts—

"The greatness of work is inside man."

—Pope John Paul II

I wish to leave my mark on the world by the quality of the relationships which I have. It is my hope that my insights and life pursuits will help others to become more closely connected to their divinity. I share the avenues I have traversed with others, and I have taken the opportunity to let my children know of my spiritual pursuits and life challenges over the years. My hope is that through my example they will find meaning to life and make choices that will bring them the gifts of the spirit and the quality of life that we all deserve.

My Thoughts—

"A useless life is an early death."

—Goethe

Today, I asked myself: What is our payoff for connecting with divinity? My inner voice said, "How about a peace that surpasses all understanding? What about total abundance and perfect health? Happiness. Joy. How about being a creator of your own world?" I must remind myself that the purpose of life is to evolve my consciousness and awareness until it becomes one with the First Cause—the Divine. Can I remember this in the midst of the challenges that I myself have created in my life?

My Thoughts—

"My life is my message."

—Mahatma Gandhi

My purpose is to manifest heaven and earth, and to do so I know I must live my life from Spirit. I must always "push the envelope" and never become complacent. My daily spiritual practices are my highest priority, and from these daily rituals, I draw upon the fire to keep me passionate and in connection with my spirit.

My Thoughts—

"The secret of success is constancy of purpose."

—Benjamin Disraeli

One of my spiritual teachers once told me that he felt each of us might have been put on this planet just to change the life of one person. This realization reminded me of what Albert Einstein once said: "A hundred times a day I remind myself that my inner and outer life are based on the labors of other men, living and dead, and that I must exert myself in order to give in the same measure as I have received."

My Thoughts—

"The way you see people is the way you treat them, and the way you treat them is what they become."

—Johann W. von Goethe

I saw a sign at a monastery today where I was conducting a workshop. It said, "The purpose of life is a life of purpose." This divine message reminded me how important it is to seek connection and meaning in how I conduct my life every day. Finding a purpose in what I do is the fuel for my motivation, passion, and enthusiasm.

My Thoughts—

"We must be the change we wish to see in the world."

—Gandhi

I read in my journal today an excerpt from my own life's mission statement. I wrote that the purpose of my work is to help people improve the quality of their lives. This statement is a wonderful reminder of the connection I feel with Spirit when I observe individuals I work with make positive changes in their lives. Writing in my journal has always helped me to remember who I am.

My Thoughts—

"The purpose of population is not ultimately peopling earth—it is to fill heaven."

—Graham Leonard

When I am teaching my time management workshops, I help people to understand that their "to do" lists should be representative of their highest priorities. What I have found with my most successful clients is that they connect their "to do" lists with a higher purpose. They find meaning in paying bills as well as in professional projects. In what areas in my life have I lost a sense of connection with what I am doing? What areas do I feel illustrate the purpose of my existence? What can I do to imbue what I do with purpose, or to weed out those things that I know do not contribute to my higher purpose?

My Thoughts—

"Some of us will live. Some of us will die. But we will all awake."

—*Restoration*

I woke up late today and felt compelled to suspend my usual routine. I usually begin my day by meditating, reading something inspirational, stretching, writing something in my journal, putting on some uplifting music, taking the dogs for a walk, and telling my wife how much I love her. Today, I pushed these things aside and instead rushed off to an appointment. I am amazed at how hard it is to remember the purpose of my work without these daily practices. Connecting with Spirit is my first priority each morning!

My Thoughts—

"Where two or more are gathered in my name, there I am . . ."

—Matthew 18:20

The majesty of life comes alive when I learn how to orient my awareness to my divine purpose. I am a body, a mind, a soul, and most importantly, Spirit. My life is truly transformed when I consciously express the power of the Divine in all of my daily and mundane routines. In what ways can I keep myself focused to remember my divinity and my purpose in each moment?

My Thoughts—

"There are two ways of spreading light: To be the candle or the mirror that reflects it."

—Edith Wharton

I am aware that there is a divine force in operation. I approach life with a renewed sense of direction and meaning. I am aware of purpose and synchronicity in my daily affairs. Synchronicity is those apparently accidental or chance events that seem to happen in my life just at the right time. Now I see the synchronicity in my day-to-day experiences as I make new connections and forge new relationships. I no longer see life as a chance occurrence but as a definite pattern of meaningful experiences. I see and feel the divine pulse in all forms of life and events.

My Thoughts—

"Everything that happens, happens as it should. There are no accidents."

—Marcus Aurelius

Each year, on the New Year, I ask myself the following questions as I begin to decide what I want to bring into my life for the year, and what I want to let go. What is my philosophy in life? What is my mission? What do I value in life? What relationships are important to me? How can I better follow my inner guidance? How can I better serve others? What thoughts and things do I want to release?

My Thoughts—

"In the long run, we only hit what we aim at."

—Henry David Thoreau

CHAPTER 4

ATTITUDE

"Everything has mind in the lead, has mind in the forefront, is made by mind. If one speaks or acts with a pure mind, happiness will follow, like a shadow that never leaves."

—The Buddha, from the *Dhammapada* (Buddhism)

This is a story of two farmers who lived next to one another. One of the farmers was your classic eternal optimist. His neighbor was quite the opposite, and was known throughout the county as Mr. Pessimist.

One morning both farmers were standing together looking at their respective properties, and the optimistic farmer was telling his friend what a glorious day it was. He was remarking that the sun was shining and that all of their crops would surely benefit from the sunlight.

The pessimist listened to his friend's comment and then turned to him and said that he did not see what was so good about the sunshine. Too much sun meant that the crops might dry up and where would they be if that happened?

The optimist looked out at the horizon and saw some dark clouds building up. He noted that it looked like it might rain by the afternoon, and would that not be wonderful? The crops would surely love a nice rainstorm.

The pessimist started shaking his head again. "Just look at the size of those storm clouds," he said. "With my luck, there's going to be too much rain and my crops will be washed out."

Now the optimist was listening to his friend and scratching his head wondering how he could help his neighbor lighten up and start looking at his glass being half full instead of half empty. So he said to his friend, "Come with me and let's do a little bird hunting." He wanted to show his friend his new hunting dog and what he could do. After some coaxing, the pessimist agreed to go along with him.

They put their rifles and the new bird dog into the truck and headed down to the lake near their properties. They got out of the truck, loaded their guns, and started walking toward the lake. Suddenly, a bird flew up into the sky, and the optimist shot the bird, and it fell into the middle of the lake.

Upon seeing the bird land in the lake, the bird dog went running across the top of the lake, brought the bird back and dropped it at his feet, and the bird dog was still completely dry. The optimist looked over at his friend and remarked, "Now have you ever seen a bird dog do that before?" The pessimist looked over at him and answered, "He probably did that because he can't swim!"

~ ~ ~ ~ ~ ~ ~ ~ ~

Like the two men in this story, you have a choice on how you want to relate to life. It helps to realize that, like the optimistic man in the story, you do not have control over how other people view a situation; you do, however, have control over how you yourself perceive it. And even though you have no control over how other people see the situation, when you are more positive you influence others to be more positive as well, just by example.

We live in a world in which we are inundated by negative messages, particularly in the media. At times, you may also have found yourself surrounded by negative people. But once you realize that you draw negativity to you by a negative attitude, you can take steps immediately to make yourself, and your world, more positive by approaching everything in your life with a positive attitude.

Attitude is a state of mind. It precedes your choice making. Although everything ultimately is a choice, you should consider identifying what the foundation of your core beliefs is everyday. Approaching life with a positive attitude is one of those prerequisites for a high quality of living. From this space, you then make choices which reflect that core belief—that positive attitude.

When you wake up knowing that your life has purpose and that you are forging a world much like a blacksmith manipulates a piece of hot iron, then you approach your day with an attitude of expectancy and anticipation as you express your divinity.

You then make choices from your state of attitude, and your world becomes a reflection of your state of being. Remember the old saying, "What goes around comes around!"

I am amazed whenever I hear the actor Christopher Reeve speak on television. Christopher was paralyzed as a result of a horseback riding incident. Told by doctors he would never walk again, Christopher has been proving all of them wrong by his progress. He said in an interview that the mind and spirit are so much stronger than the body. He is a prime example of someone whose attitude is reflective of his ability to express his divinity.

My Thoughts—

"Never, never, never, never give up"

—Winston Churchill

When someone asks how I am, I will respond: "I am perfect." For I *am* perfect. I am a divine being. I accept this fact now, and I approach everything and everyone in my life as if they are a divine being. My legacy as a divine being makes me perfect; my legacy as a human being brings the gifts of choice and mistake, to allow me to make choices and to learn. I am perfect, but not perfect in everything I do—yet!

My Thoughts—

"The confidence we have in others stems directly from our confidence in ourselves."

—Francois, Duc de La Rochefoucauld

If I want a more joyful life, I must change my limiting attitudes and beliefs. When I desire union with my higher self—my divinity—more than anything else, then everything else I desire will manifest fully. I now close the door to the past. There is only the now. Life is magical.

My Thoughts—

"Renew thyself completely each day; do it again, and again, forever again."

—Chinese Inscription

I know that the intensity with which I desire something has great power to help me realize my desires. One of the ways I can increase the intensity of my thoughts is through conviction. If I can with conviction—with certainty and with strong belief—direct my thoughts and actions toward positive outcomes in my life, then truly my search for my divinity and lasting inner peace will be a living reality for me. Conviction is an element of a positive attitude.

My Thoughts—

"The most important tool for success is the belief that you can succeed."

—Author Unknown

My life is a reflection of my thoughts. Like a garden, whatever I plant is what I reap, whether the seed is planted in the inner garden of my thoughts or in the soil of the world around me by my words and actions. All of creation was formed according to an idea, and I too have the capability to plant seeds and create the world I want. What seeds do I want to plant to honor my spirit?

My Thoughts—

"If your mind isn't clogged by unnecessary things, this is the best season of your life."

—Author Unknown

I speak, think, and act positively, and the Universe responds in kind. I absolutely refuse to indulge in negative emotions and thoughts, and I think and act only on what I want to create in my life.

My Thoughts—

"They can because they think they can."

—Virgil

What I focus on is what I attract in my life. For that reason, I need to remind myself to make a list of persons, events and things which have brought and continue to bring joy and love into my life. The next time I am feeling angry or upset about something, I want to remember to switch my thoughts to something on my "feel good" list. When I am successful at doing this, my negative thoughts and feelings disappear.

My Thoughts—

"The greatest discovery is that a human being can alter his life by altering his attitudes of mind."

—William James

I heard on the radio today about a robber who held up a small grocery. He was about to leave the store with his stolen goods, which included beer, when the store clerk had the nerve to mention that all customers carrying beer out of the store needed to be over twenty-one. "I am over twenty-one!" the criminal said, and to prove it pulled out his license, showed it to the clerk and then left the store. The clerk called the police and reported the robber's name, and as a result, the police caught him. When I heard this story, I could not stop laughing. When I laugh, I have noticed my attitude improves, I feel myself relax, and it seems the world is a bit brighter. Laughing is good for my attitude. What situations make you laugh?

My Thoughts—

"No one would have been invited to dinner as often as Jesus unless he was interesting and had a sense of humor."

—Author Unknown

I enjoy love and laughter more than I enjoy pain and sorrow. Even so, pain and sorrow have their uses; they help me grow. I need to remember that the challenges I attract are also my gifts. God is teaching me in both the good times and the bad. Where I have forgotten this fact in my life? In what situations have I recognized the gifts of my challenges?

My Thoughts—

"Above all, life should be fun."

—Author Unknown

I spend a great deal of time trying to keep my physical environment in order—my desk, my car, my yard, etc. Perhaps I should apply "cleaning my house" to the mental and emotional places inside myself. For example, I forgave both of my parents years ago for some of the emotional trauma that I perceived them as having inflicted on me. The result of doing this actually improved our relationship in their latter years before they passed away. Do I have some beliefs that need to be reexamined? Is it time to reassess some of my goals? Are there people I still need to reconnect with or forgive?

My Thoughts—

"Get the better of yourself—this is the best kind of victory."

—Miguel De Cervantes

Scientists say people use only four to six percent of their brain capacity. If that is true, then what is my true potential? If everyone has the capacity for living a highly creative and fulfilling life, then what keeps us from achieving such a life? I believe that the obstacles that keep me from achieving a creative and fulfilling life are self-imposed limitations like worry, anxiety, or fear. I will work to remove these influences from my life, and enjoy the benefits of doing so.

My Thoughts—

"I always entertain great hopes."

—Robert Frost

In living a spiritual life, I measure my achievement differently than I have measured achievement in my life. I have clients who have earned tremendous wealth and prestige in their lives, yet they are unhappy. They have tried to bring happiness into the lives by reaching outside themselves. When I practice living spiritually, I approach life from the inside out with an attitude of being connected with Spirit. Spirit brings me a sense of fulfillment, and from that place I can then reach out into the world for all the material things I deserve.

My Thoughts—

"The empires of the future are the empires of the mind."

—Winston Churchill

I was told by a wise teacher that one of the keys to life was adopting an attitude of *spiritual indifference* and *emotional detachment* in all situations. By *spiritual indifference*, he meant being able to see all people and circumstances—their happiness and pain, their rewards and their challenges and disappointments—as a divine unfoldment and the result of choices that individual made. By *emotional detachment*, he was not saying not to be compassionate or empathic toward people. He was trying to show me that every person is experiencing what they've drawn to themselves so they can grow, and each soul is evolving through the choices that person has made. They are experiencing a divine process of growth and change, just as I am. I must not let someone else's challenges affect my own attitude.

My Thoughts—

"The really happy person is one who can enjoy the scenery on a detour."

—Anonymous

When I find I need to change my attitude, I ask myself the following questions: What are the strong points of my personality, and am I living my life according to these traits? What do I need to work on and what I am doing about it? A change in attitude is about self-care. Self-care means first building a good relationship with myself, so I can then have good relationships with others and be a positive force in their lives.

My Thoughts—

"We must learn to reawaken and keep ourselves awake, not by mechanical aids, but by an infinite expectation of the dawn."

—Thoreau

I have discovered one of the secrets to manifesting whatever I want in my life: *desire*. I decide what I truly desire, and I allow myself to feel that desire, to yearn for it. Once I know what I desire, and commit to it through my emotions, change comes into my life.

My Thoughts—

"To achieve, you must believe something and want something with all of your might. Then, you must be willing to commit yourself to a course."

—Author Unknown

I can be guided by Spirit in each moment wherever I go. I just need to remember to ask. Spirit withholds nothing from me. This is my belief. This is how I approach my life, and what I teach others to consider.

My Thoughts—

"We are what we believe we are."

—Benjamin Cardozo

CHAPTER 5

CHOICE

"But seek ye first the kingdom of God, and his righteousness; and all things shall be added unto you."

—Matthew 6:10 (Christianity)

I was sent this story by a friend; the author is unknown. The story's main character is a man named Jerry. He was the kind of guy you would love to emulate. Jerry was always in a good mood and had something positive to say. When someone would ask him how he was doing, he would reply, "If I were any better, I would be twins."

Jerry owned a restaurant and was considered a unique manager. Because he had a great attitude and was a natural motivator, several of his waiters followed him whenever he purchased a new restaurant. People responded to his positive attitude. If one of his employees was having a bad day, he was there helping the employee look on the positive side of the situation.

Seeing Jerry's style made one of his patrons curious, and one day he went up to Jerry and said, "I don't get it. You can't be a positive person all of the time. How do you do it?"

Jerry replied, "Each morning I wake up and say to myself, 'Jerry you have two *choices* today. You can choose to be in a good mood or you can choose to be in a bad mood. I choose to be in a good mood. Each time something bad happens, I can choose to be a victim or I can choose to learn from it. I choose to learn from it. Every time someone comes to me complaining, I can choose to accept their complaining or I can point out the positive side of life. I choose the positive side of life.'"

"You make it sound easy," replied the patron, "but it's not."

"Yes, it is!" Jerry said. "Life is all about choices. When you cut away all of the junk, every situation is a choice. You can choose how you react to situations. You can choose how people affect your mood. The bottom line is: It's your choice how you live life."

The patron reflected on what Jerry had said. Soon after, the patron moved out of town and lost touch with Jerry. But the patron often thought about Jerry and began to make a conscious choice about life instead of just reacting to it.

Several years later, the patron heard a story about Jerry doing something you are never supposed to do in a restaurant business: He left the back door open one morning. Three armed robbers entered the restaurant and held him up at gunpoint. While trying to open the safe, Jerry's hand, shaking from nervousness, slipped off the combination. The robbers apparently panicked and shot him.

Luckily, Jerry was found relatively quickly and rushed to the local trauma center. After eighteen hours of surgery and weeks of intensive care, Jerry was released from the hospital with fragments of the bullets still in his body.

The patron saw Jerry about six months after the accident. When he asked Jerry how he was, Jerry replied, "If I was any better, I would be twins. Wanna see my scars?" The patron declined to see the wounds but did ask him what had gone through his mind as the robbery took place.

"The first thing that went through my mind was that I should have locked the back door," Jerry replied. "Then, as I lay on the floor, I remembered that I had two choices. I could choose to live, or I could choose to die. I chose to live," he continued.

The patron responded, "Weren't you scared? Did you lose consciousness?" Jerry said, "The paramedics were great. They kept telling me I was going to be fine. But when they wheeled me into the emergency room and I saw the expressions on the faces of the doctors and nurses, I got really scared. In their eyes, I could tell they thought I was a dead man. I knew I needed to take action."

The patron asked Jerry what he did. With a big smile Jerry said, "Well, there was a big, burly nurse shouting questions at me. She asked if I was allergic to anything. I told her yes. I then saw the doctors and nurses stop working as they waited for my reply. I took a deep breath and yelled, 'Bullets!' Over their laughter, I told them I am choosing to live. 'Operate on me as if I am going to live, not die.'"

Jerry lived, thanks to the skill of the doctors, but also because of his amazing attitude. His story can teach all of us a valuable lesson: that every day we have the choice to live fully. This attribute of free will—the ability to choose in each moment—is also part of your divine inheritance which I talked about earlier in the book. *Every* choice you make causes a corresponding effect. This is spiritual law! No one is exempt from the repercussions of this spiritual law. So choose wisely!

Purpose has always been the fuel that puts my intentions into action. I feel a connection with Spirit when I am aware that everything I do each day can have a higher meaning—a higher purpose—when I choose to see it that way. From performing a kind act to doing something for myself, each moment can be filled with purpose. Seeking purpose and meaning in my day is one of the choices I make that enriches my life.

My Thoughts—

"Life itself can't give you joy,
Unless you really will it;
Life just gives you time and space,
It's up to you to fill it."

—Author Unknown

God gave us the power of choice. If collectively, as a race, we choose fear over love, then we lose our connection to our divinity. Such is the challenge that we face today as a human race. There are always consequences for our actions and the choices we make. Therefore, if the majority of the human race were making choices from a place of love, can you imagine what that would mean? We would be creating heaven on earth.

My Thoughts—

"Destiny is not a matter of chance, it is a matter of choice. It is not a thing to be waited for; it is a thing to be achieved."

—William Jennings Bryan

I was reading the newspaper today, and it seemed the entire paper was about child abuse, child abduction, corporate scandal, the possibility of war, robbery, and gang shootings. Every one of these things reflects choices people made. What type of choices would people make if they were truly in touch with their divinity? Because I am a divine being who is omnipresent (everywhere present at once), then when I make a positive change, the entire world is affected in some way by my choice. What situations are impacted around me when I make choices that reflect the divinity within me?

My Thoughts—

"Humanity is being taken to the point where it will have to choose between suicide and adoration."

—Sri Aurobindo

When one looks at all the forms of life that exist on this planet, from the one cell microorganisms to the human realm, there is an attribute humans possess that no other form of life does. That attribute is the power of conscious choice. In the animal kingdom, choice is, for the most part, made by instinct. For us as humans (and divine beings), choice involves taking in information, internalizing it, making a decision about what we want to do, and observing ourselves acting on the choices we have made. I want to make good, conscious choices in each moment.

My Thoughts—

"The strongest principle of growth lies in the human choice."

—George Eliot

I realize that I sometimes make choices based upon previous experiences I have had in my life. I have made choices out of fear and ignorance. There have been times that my worries about money caused me to change jobs for the wrong reasons. My stubbornness in listening to the advice of others caused me to make poor decisions. Where have I made poor choices in my life and what do I need to do to stop myself from continuing to make such choices? What good choices have I made?

My Thoughts—

"Assert your right to make a few mistakes. Mistakes are the lesson of wisdom."

—Author Unknown

The way we see life can be compared to a slide projector and a screen. The screen is what we see as life in our outer world; the projector is our brain, filtering our internal perception through our eyes. If I put a slide into my projector, such as love, a corresponding picture is illuminated on my screen (my outer world)— a picture of love. I look at the slide as a choice I am making in what I will concentrate on. Then what situations I am attracting in life are a reflection of my focus.

My Thoughts—

"I know of no more encouraging fact than the unquestionable ability of man to elevate his life by conscious endeavor."

—Thoreau

Perhaps the Divine's intent in giving me the power of choice is to enable me to create the world of my choice. That power of choice has a double edge to it. I can create great joy in my life, or I can erect tremendous roadblocks for myself. Science says that for every cause there is an effect. I need to remember that each choice I make will have an effect in my life. Do I want to attract joy or pain? What can I do to attract those things I want in my life?

My Thoughts—

"The universe is transformation—our life is what our thoughts make it."

—Marcus Aurelius

Everything I believe is based on my perception. I act on every perception by making a choice. Choice is an attitude. For example, if I believe that all forms of life are an expression of the Divine and this belief is a foundation of my attitude, then I should choose to treat everyone with respect and dignity. Not doing so could create problems for myself like a strained relationship. So I need to choose wisely. I need to speak from my heart after contemplation. Do my words and actions create harmony or do they create division?

My Thoughts—

"All that is needed to make a happy life is within yourself, in your way of thinking."

—Marcus Aurelius

My life and the choices I make must be based in truth, in love, and in compassion. Free will grants me the freedom to do so, but free will also allows me to do harm to someone. But there are consequences when I do so. I am conscious of the need to show love and compassion in the choices I make. How can I expand my consciousness to embrace positive choice making?

My Thoughts—

"Most people are about as happy as they make up their minds to be."

—Abraham Lincoln

I told a friend that I feel that we are truly divine beings. His response was to question me, saying "Then why are we human beings? What was the purpose of our human experience if we were divine beings?" I told him that being human gives us the opportunity to practice our choice making in order to unfold and discover our divinity. What I realized after talking to him was that he believes that God is in the sky—not within himself. I respect and understand that this is his choice and that he has a right to this perception. I hope that he will grant me the same freedom of choice without judgment.

My Thoughts—

"Achievement comes when you decide to live your possibilities."

—Author Unknown

Sometimes I struggle on issues and debate on what I should do. There are times that I react too quickly and make a poor choice. The bottom line for myself is this: I choose Spirit's way instead of weighing choices and consequences. When I do have to analyze the pros and cons of a situation, I ask Spirit. There is only one way—the way of Spirit. I choose the way of Spirit. I am learning to recognize how Spirit communicates with me. I am also learning to ask for guidance more often.

My Thoughts—

"Choose your own path."

—Unknown

The two most powerful words in the English language are "yes" and "no." I say "yes" to any choices which create harmony in my relationships. I say "yes" to thoughts of love and joy. I say "no" to any thoughts and actions which might cause harm to someone. The quality of my life is based on these choices. This is true empowerment. Where do I need to improve my choice making? What areas of my life should I say "yes" to, and in what areas should I say "no"?

My Thoughts—

"Hold yourself responsible for a higher standard than anyone else expects of you. Never excuse yourself."

—Henry Ward Beecher

I spend a great deal of time in my workshops emphasizing the power of choice. The challenge for me is to help individuals understand that if you can visualize something you want, really feel and desire it, and take actions to make it happen, then you can bring anything you want into your life. Many people come to my workshops unaware that they have the power to make such a choice; and some leave my workshops unwilling to make such a change and begin making such choices. For some reason, people choose to not make the effort to improve their lives. This is their choice, and though it is not mine, I respect it.

My Thoughts—

"Things do not happen. Things are made to happen."

—John F. Kennedy

I was asked today whether I felt the United States was going to war with Iraq. I told the person who asked the question that I believe war is always avoidable. I believe there is a peaceful solution to any conflict when we choose to envision peace instead of conflict. I mistrust the true intentions of those in our government who are always advocating war. Peace is a choice. So is protecting ourselves, if necessary.

My Thoughts—

"Two roads diverged in a wood, and I
I took the one less traveled by,
and that has made all the difference."

—Robert Frost

CHAPTER 6

ABUNDANCE

"I am the vine, ye are the branches. He that abideth in me, and I in him, the same bringeth forth much fruit: for without me ye can do nothing."

—John 15:1 (Christianity)

I magine in your mind's eye that there are three individuals standing in the desert, and it is pitch dark. In fact, it is so dark that they cannot even see their hands in front of their faces. These individuals have been lost in the desert for some time trying to find their trail back home.

Each has an Arabian stallion, and each is holding onto the harness of the horse.

Suddenly, out of the darkness comes a voice which they have never heard, yet at the same time, it is unmistakable. It is the voice of the Creator, the Almighty Divine. "Pick up the pebbles around you," comes the command from his Holiness.

Although the three men have been scared at times, they always kept traveling. Their horses are as tired as the three of them are. But the voice is unmistakable, and they feel compelled to follow its commands. They get down on their hands and knees, and they begin to grope around for pebbles, grabbing a few and grumbling about what they are doing. The voice then says, "Mount your horses and ride until dawn. There you will find yourself in a place where you will be happy, and where you will also be sad." They look at each other wondering what the Creator means, but again, they feel compelled to obey.

As they ride into the darkness, each is filled with many questions as well as anticipation as to what the dawn will bring. They have put the pebbles into their pockets, and while riding they talk to each other, wondering aloud what the pebbles mean and what they will look like in the light of the dawn.

As the sun appears on the horizon and its first light strikes the men, they stop and dismount from their horses and realize they made it home. They circle around each other and take the pebbles out of their pockets. The light of the sun strikes the pebbles, and suddenly, they are surrounded by wonderful colors radiating from the pebbles, which they realize are diamonds, sapphires, emeralds, and rubies.

They look at each other and realize the meaning of what the Creator has said to them. They are happy that they picked up the pebbles, but they are sad because they did not pick up more!

⌐ ⌐ ⌐ ⌐ ⌐ ⌐ ⌐ ⌐ ⌐

How often have you been wandering around in the desert of your life wishing you had something—a well-paying job, a fulfilling relationship, perfect health, or some material thing? This story is a reminder that you have everything you need now if you are willing to pay attention and listen. Ideas, inspirations, people, money, all events in your life—all are part of the abundance which is available to you.

Abundance is not just about prosperity. Abundance is about an attitude and an awareness that everything in our lives has a divine origin. How often do you miss some of the pebbles that have been given to you by events which you are attracting in your life? How many times have you found yourself feeling lost in some of your life pursuits, instead of recognizing the lessons and gifts being given to you, in every moment?

What would you do if the voice of the Creator spoke to you and indicated some task that he wished you to pursue? Would you listen? Would you recognize the voice?

Be assured that, without a doubt, the Divine and his many helpers are sending messages and signals to you all of the time. His instruction can come through people or circumstances, in situations both positive and negative. His loving message can come in the form of hunches or in other ways.

Abundance has many synonyms which can assist you,

understanding that everything you could possibly desire in your life has already been given. Some of these synonyms are: plenty, surplus, bountiful, profusion, enough, and overflowing.

Recognizing abundance at work in your life is one of the most important things you can learn to do. Once you have begun recognizing abundance, you will soon become eternally grateful for having everything you need supplied to you on a moment-by-moment basis. You will also learn to state your intention through desire and commitment, for those things you desire for yourself. Become internally and externally vigilant and know that you are never alone on your journey.

My prosperity is only an aspect of my abundance. Making money can at times make me focus on the effects instead of the cause. True abundance is a recognition of where all things spring from, and that is a realization that Spirit is responsible for the true cause of what manifests in my life. In what areas of my life am I concentrating only on the effects and not the cause?

My Thoughts—

"There is no wealth, but life."

—John Ruskin

One of my spiritual teachers gave me a key to manifestation: acceptance. He said that we are taught, for the most part, that our lives are about learning how to give. He said that some of us have become master givers. Now we need to become master receivers. If whatever I need has already been given, then acceptance is the bridge which brings it to me.

My Thoughts—

"Believe. That's all you must do; just believe."

—Author Unknown

I know I am living an abundant life when I can discern the lessons in the challenges that I attract. Whatever I am presented with in life is what I need. It is easy for me to feel abundant when things are going well. My challenge is to recognize the worth of the challenges I'm given, and to recognize the abundance offered me through them.

My Thoughts—

"Grasp the opportunity to manage change; not avoid it.
Change is the very essence of life."

—Author Unknown

I realize how much consciousness and attitude are elements of abundance. Things do not come true until I accept what I want in my consciousness. Acceptance is an attitude. And my attitude is one of abundance. What is exciting to me about these realizations is that no one on this planet is excluded from being nurtured, abundantly. Knowledge is truly power!

My Thoughts—

"Know where you started. From there, you can go anywhere."

—Author Unknown

If I am conscious of abundance and its effects, then I see the Divine in all aspects of life. My divine inheritance can mean whatever I choose for it to mean, and it can represent anything I desire in my life. Then my abundant attitude must be able to see what I desire, live it, and feel it. And then I realize abundance in my life. My abundant attitude also has one other important ingredient to it: gratitude. I say "Thank You" often! Who and what is an element of abundance in my life?

My Thoughts—

"Be glad of life because it gives you the chance to love and to work and to play and to look at the stars."

—Author Unknown

Symbolically speaking, when I hold an empty cup up to the Universe, I am suggesting that I lack something. I hold a full cup up to the Universe. I acknowledge my desires. Just because something has not manifested physically does not mean that it has not been given. How and when things come into manifestation is one of many divine mysteries. When have you felt abundance was lacking in your life, only to recognize later that abundance had already begun to manifest without your recognition of it?

My Thoughts—

"The sun shines not on us, but in us."

—John Muir

If I want to produce beauty in my life, I must surround myself with beauty. But I must do so both internally and externally. Outwardly, I am conscious of beauty around me. Inwardly, when I meditate, I can concentrate on the beauty of my inner world. The more I look for beauty within and without, the more beauty I attract. Today, I will make a list of what beauty I see.

My Thoughts—

"Live each season as it passes; breathe the air, drink the drink, taste the fruit—and enjoy the influences of each."

—Thoreau

I realized today that living a life filled with grace is the outward expression of the harmony which exists within me. It comes from a place of holiness. I can live my life in grace, or I can live my life by experience. Experience is the student. Grace is the teacher. I like to be a teacher most of the time, and I always choose to be a student when appropriate.

My Thoughts—

"Make life as meaningful as possible."

—Author Unknown

Thank you, God, for a most fabulous life. With your omnipresence, I always have abundance. I accept my abundance as my divinity, and I totally accept all that I desire in my life. I do not take anything for granted, and I look for ways to share my abundance.

My Thoughts—

"The spirit of life unites everyone and makes possible a world of peace, joy, and love."

—Author Unknown

My massage therapist, who is not only a healer but an individual who is gifted spiritually, reminded me gently today that anytime I make transitions in my work, I tend to concentrate on the money. This was a nice reminder that I need to concentrate on Spirit. Working is about love, not money. The fact that I attract so many individuals whom I look at as my teachers is such a wonderful gift from Spirit.

My Thoughts—

"It is for us to make the effort. The result is in God's hands."

—Author Unknown

A very well-known intuitive and spiritual counselor told me once that I will always have money around me and attract it to me when I understand the source of my true wealth. He said I will probably give most of it away. Prosperity is about flow. Beyond prosperity, I now know that abundance is an all-inclusive supply of whatever is needed to give me a fulfilling life.

My Thoughts—

"Self-trust is the first secret of success."

—Ralph Waldo Emerson

We sometimes block a more abundant attitude by concentrating on the form. When I do so, I lose about eighty percent of my power. One hundred percent of my attention should be on Spirit. Then I can look at matter or manifestation from its true source. Each day I need to ask myself: What is the essence of what I am viewing in this moment?

My Thoughts—

"If you want to get the best out of someone, you must look for the best that is in them."

—Author Unknown

The good news about abundance is that it does not require us to depend upon someone else to provide us with what we want or need. Abundance comes to us apart from our employer, our parents, our friends, or even our government. We are truly free when we realize that our consciousness is our abundance. Whatever your mind can conceive of is what you will receive. This is also a spiritual law.

My Thoughts—

"Nurture your mind with great thoughts; heroes are made by believing."

—Benjamin Disraeli

CHAPTER 7

COURAGE

"Everything is laid out for you. Your path is straight ahead
of you. Sometimes it's invisible but it's there. You may not
know where it's going but you have to follow that path. It's
the path to the creator. It's the only path there is."

—Chief Lean Shenandoah (Native American)

Sometimes, in our darkest hours when we feel there is no hope, God sends us a messenger who opens an inner door and brings light into our hearts. Such it was in the story that Bill told me one day. Bill is one of my most trusted clients, and he told me he has only been able to tell this story to one other person in his life.

The story begins with Bill, his wife and his two children moving to San Antonio from Rochester, New York. He was starting a new job, and they decided to live in an apartment for a couple of months before moving into their new house. Five weeks later, Bill's life took a sudden turn. His wife announced that she wanted a divorce.

Though Bill and his wife had been having what he felt were the usual marital problems, he was stunned by her announcement. In the next weeks, their marriage began to unravel quickly, and Bill was forced to move out. Sitting alone in his own apartment one night in the dark, he began to hear various voices filling his head, causing him worry, fear, and anger.

Would he be able to see his children again and would he be able to tuck them in at night? Would his wife decide to move back to Rochester or somewhere else far away, taking his children from where Bill's new job and career now were? Bill not only struggled with worry, but he also felt filled with guilt. He realized that he had not been the best husband, but how could he go on without being a father?

In the next weeks, Bill's children were shuffled back and forth between their parents. Bill learned that his wife had met someone else and wanted to move to another city. Would she demand that the kids move with her? Would he be comfortable with the new boyfriend that she had found?

Finally, in utter desperation, Bill turned to the only anchor he had in his life: his church. He began to spend hours in church praying for courage and asking that he not be separated from his kids. One day in church something occurred that changed his life forever.

He was attending his usual Sunday mass, and that day the church was full. Bill took a seat in a pew with someone sitting to his left, and leaving an open space to his right where someone else might sit.

Bill told me that he prayed and listened to the sermon, all the while thinking of his children, and regretting anything he might have done that had led to his divorce. He said when the service was almost over and he knelt down for the final prayer, he noticed out of the corner of his eye an elderly lady sitting in the space next to his right. He wondered how she had gotten there, since he had not seen anyone entering the pew and sitting down.

When Bill sat back in his seat, he looked at the woman again. She had beautiful white hair that matched her white pants suit. His eyes met hers, and he sensed an indescribable presence about her.

Suddenly the woman grabbed Bill's hand with both of her hands, looked him in the eye and, with an expression of intense love, told Bill, "Now you go out there and have a good day and take one day at a time." Bill was simultaneously touched and stunned by her comment. He noticed everyone else standing so he pulled his hand away from the grasp of the elderly lady and stood up.

Standing, he turned to help the lady out of her seat, but she was gone. Bill looked hurriedly behind him and in all directions, but the woman was nowhere to be seen. In that moment, he then realized that no one would find this woman, as she had been sent by God on this day to deliver a message to Bill.

That very special day, Bill felt his penance was over. He knew he could move forward in his life. It was time to move on in many ways—to forgive his wife and, most of all, to forgive himself. With the help of God in the guise of an elderly stranger, Bill had found the *courage* to start his new life. As a wonderful footnote to this story, he ended up getting custody of his children, and today lives very happily with his new wife, a fulfilling career, and a deep love for God.

Courage is that quality we all possess that gives us the inner strength to face the various challenges we attract to ourselves. Courage is what we draw upon to live our truth regardless of what others think. It is courage that enables us to finally surrender our humanity and accept our divinity.

In the Native American culture, there are references made to our dark times when we are confronted with various challenges and choices. In that tradition, it is said that "when the dark clouds are blowing, you just have to push your way through." This takes courage, especially when the winds are blowing hard. When have I felt the dark winds blowing in my own life, and, guided by courage, what did I do to push through?

My Thoughts—

"You gain strength, courage, and confidence by every experience in which you stop to look fear in the face."

—Eleanor Roosevelt

I have a lot of respect for social, political, and environmental activists who are willing to express and act on their views in spite of conventional opinion. Until each of us is acting from our spirit, we need others who can help us see when our choices are not of Spirit, but are self-serving. Community gives us fellow travelers as we walk the path that connects us with Spirit. Where do I need to become more involved with my community? What do I really believe in, and am I willing to express my truth no matter what?

My Thoughts—

"It is our task—our essential, central, crucial task—to transform ourselves from mere social creatures into community creatures. It is the only way human evolution will be able to proceed."

—Scott Peck

As a parent, I must have the courage and the faith to allow my children to choose the path they wish to follow, and forge it themselves. Letting go of what I think my kids should be is truly an act of unconditional love. I must have the courage to allow them to make choices, help them if they will allow me, and let them fall once in a while. They, too, are divine beings with a purpose to fulfill.

My Thoughts—

"To persevere, trusting in what you hope for, is courage."

—Euripedes

There was a time in my life when my parents did not want to have anything to do with me. At that time, I had a very different belief system than did my parents, and they strongly disagreed with how I was living my life. When they finally realized that I was living a good life and they had no control over me, we mended our relationship. I honor my parents, but I do not have to live my life to fulfill their expectations. It was hard for me to stand my ground until they gave up wanting to control my life, and it took courage to do so, in spite of the possible consequences.

My Thoughts—

"Those who cannot hear the music think the dancers mad."

—Anonymous

Today, someone asked me what my own religious affiliation was, since I talk about God and Jesus often. I told the person who asked that I am not part of any church or group by choice. Although I respect traditional religion, I consider myself to be a spiritual person with no ties to any tradition or dogma. I have studied many of the world's greatest spiritual teachers, and I enjoy Jesus' teachings. I listen to the voice of the Divine within me, rather than going by the guidelines of an organization. Even though the path I have chosen seems to perplex some of my traditional religious friends, I remain faithful to my beliefs and values which takes courage at times.

My Thoughts—

"It is better to die on your feet than to live on your knees."

—Dolores Ibarriuri

Recently, I felt one of my clients was behaving inappropriately, and I felt I needed to confront him. He had fallen into a habit of saying negative things about people behind their backs. I had observed this habit growing in him, and I finally decided I had to say something about it, and had to gather the courage to do so, knowing that he might not handle the feedback well. When I told him I did not agree with his habit and felt it was detrimental to his growth, his reaction was not favorable. But I felt it was necessary to speak out, because, as a member of his community, I felt I needed to do my part to help him act from his divine spirit. Being truthful in these situations takes courage.

My Thoughts—

"And the trouble is, if you don't risk anything, you risk even more."

—Erica Jong

I affirm each day that I am willing to stand up for my truth regardless of the consequences. I know that life will teach me by sending me lessons that will either affirm the accuracy of my truth or show me a higher way of looking at things. Who have I been afraid to share by truth with in the past, and why?

My Thoughts—

"I will judge my successes by how well I live my truth, not by how well my truth is received."

—Andre Gide

I have been having difficulty with one of my clients whose humor sends mixed messages. The underlying message of his humorous remarks is that he does not respect what I do. I have been reluctant to confront him, and on reflection I realized fear was behind my lack of action. I discovered that I do not like confronting people when I feel conflict with them. I have discovered how fear and courage are tied to one another—I want to be more aware of things I resist, and ask myself if fear is at work, and if courage is called for. I know this person came into my life to help me learn this lesson.

My Thoughts—

"What you are, the world is. And without your transformation there can be no transformation of the world."

—J. Krishnamurti

My daughter told me today that one of her friends asked for help in running away from her parents. My daughter told her no, and that she should go home and work things out with her parents. When some of my daughter's friends heard what she did, they chastised her for not helping out. My daughter's response was that it would have been wrong to do so. She has learned the power of the word *no*. My daughter's courage inspires me, and I told her so.

My Thoughts—

"It is not the critic that counts. The credit belongs to the one who is actually in the arena; who strives valiantly."

—Theodore Roosevelt

This week I told all of my clients that I would be ending my consulting relationship with them in three months. I have felt that I cannot advance them any further, and I need to move on. My wife and I discussed the possible financial consequences, and we also realized that Spirit was suggesting that it was time for a change. In these moments, I feel very connected with Spirit, and I also feel anxiety. I have become aware how much courage it takes to let Spirit guide my life totally.

My Thoughts—

"We shall not cease from exploration and the end of all our exploring will be to arrive where we started and to know the place for the first time."

—T. S. Eliot

I was asked today what I felt the difference was between courage and faith. My answer was that I believe that courage needs to happen first in my consciousness. My desire to risk and follow guidance takes courage. Faith happens after I have taken a courageous step. Faith allows me to know that God will fulfill my intentions once I have decided to proceed forward.

My Thoughts—

"So plunge into the truth, find out who the teacher is, believe in the great sound!"

—Kabir

I am reminded often that as a teacher I must be willing to plant seeds even though I know I may not see my plants grow. At times, I have questioned whether my work is assisting individuals in their lives. But my only real job is to live a life directed by Spirit. I may not always know what good things such a life brings. Am I living and teaching my truth or am I looking for confirmation from others?

My Thoughts—

"Great people are those who make others feel that they, too, can become great."

—Mark Twain

Each day I gain courage in my convictions. I walk tall and firm in Spirit knowing that there is only one truth: that I am of Spirit, and that I deserve to be happy and fulfilled.

My Thoughts—

"And the day came when the risk to remain tight in a bud was more painful than the risk it took to blossom."

—Anais Nin

When the day comes that you truly decide to accept your divinity, let go of your humanity and turn your life over to Spirit, this day will test the very fiber of your soul. You will face your deepest fears, and in that space, you will find your true self.

My Thoughts—

"Twenty years from now you will be more disappointed by the things that you didn't do than by the one you did do. So throw off the bowlines. Sail away from the safe harbors. Catch the trade winds in your sails. Explore. Dream."

—Mark Twain

CHAPTER 8

FAITH

"So through spiritual wisdom, dear one, we come to know that all life is one. In the beginning was only Being, one without a second."

—from the *Chandogya Upanishad* (Hinduism)

S everal years ago I found myself in a workshop, sitting at a table with a group of people. One of the women at the table began telling the group about a church in San Francisco. She called it the Church for the Homeless, even though all types of people attended it including actors Robin Williams and Sharon Stone.

She described the church, its services and its mission so touchingly that we were all in tears by the time she had finished telling us about it. I was so moved by her description of it that I made a note to visit this church if I should ever have the opportunity to travel to the Bay Area.

I think that note was all it took to put the wheels of synchronicity in motion. So, about two years later, I found myself with a client in the Bay Area, and planning a business trip to San Francisco. In planning it, I made sure that I stayed through a Sunday so I could visit this church and attend its services.

I flew to San Francisco, met with my client, and began asking people I met about Glide Memorial United Methodist Church. People seemed to know the church; they said it was in downtown San Francisco. Everyone I asked about Glide Memorial spoke with such feeling about this church that I was even more intrigued. That Sunday, with anticipation and great expectancy, I drove through the various downtown streets until I came upon a huge three-story building which looked, in part, like an old house.

I drove up to one of the men in orange vests directing traffic, and found he was not a policeman, as I had expected, but one of the homeless people who donated their services on Sundays. He parked cars for those coming to the service. He told me to give him my keys, and he would park my car. Part of me thought: Give my keys to a homeless person? But my inner voice told me to have faith. I remembered that the woman I had met in the workshop had told me the church tested people's faith. Although I was unsure, I made the choice to turn my rental car, which had my luggage and other travel possessions in the back seat, over to a complete stranger.

As I got out of my car, I saw a huge line of people around the church. They were homeless people waiting to be fed in the church's basement. I felt as if I was a movie star. I could see the people waiting in line looking at me. I felt my defenses go up immediately as I thought about my safety. The walk from my car to the front of the church seemed like a long one. I walked into the church and climbed a couple of flights of stairs and entered the main room where the service would be held.

The church was almost full that day. I saw a piano, drums and electric guitars. On the wall above the stage, slides of children and church outreach activities were being projected. I took a seat, and then sixty or so people in ordinary street clothes walked onto the stage. They looked much like the people I'd seen in the food lines outside.

The reverend entered the room, the choir started singing, the band started up, and in moments everyone in the room were standing, clapping and singing. The slides on the wall mirrored the message of the song in words and pictures.

For the next hour I was transported to another dimension. As the preacher was delivering his sermon, slides projected pictures that reinforced his message onto the wall above him. The choir slowly hummed a tune while he was talking. Everyone participated, everyone contributed. The atmosphere was absolutely magical. And as if the atmosphere were not magical enough, that day the reverend delivered a message that had a great deal of impact on me. His message was about faith.

The reverend said that faith was not something we talk about, but it is something we practice. "Don't talk about your faith," he said, "live it." He then talked about the growth of Glide Memorial in its early days. He talked about how the church found ways to form outreach ministries, even though there was no money. He talked about how, week after week, the church's overhead was more than it was taking in.

"But we knew that the church's needs would be met," he said, "and they were." He said the church members knew, even in those early days, that Glide Memorial would touch thousands of people with its message.

He asked the congregation several questions that morning. "Are you willing to live what you believe in even if there are people around who disapprove of what you do?" he asked. "Are you willing to practice your faith when things are not going well for you? Are you letting your mind wander in your low moments, losing faith and questioning whether something you need will happen in your life?"

The reverend concluded his sermon by saying it was time for us to reclaim the glory of heaven. He said we needed a "new time religion." And he said that Glide would be a church for all ethnic groups, all sexual preferences, and for those whose wealth was abundant and those who were in need. No one would be excluded.

He remarked that Glide Memorial was faith put into action. By its very commitment, it would challenge those in the community who were prejudiced, biased, or who held particular dogmas. Those people would likely shun Glide for its spiritual position. But that was a small price to pay for the glory living such a mission would bring.

I came away from my experience with Glide Memorial inspired, and resolved to deepen my faith. That sermon reinforced that my faith is representative of my beliefs, my convictions, and my trust and certainty that I am a divine being, and that I am never alone or without anything I need to live a fulfilling and purposeful life.

As one of the parking attendants delivered my car to me, I just knew everything was okay. He looked at me and said, "It's been a pleasure serving you. Thank you for having faith in me." I smiled and said, "I should be the one thanking you." We shook hands and I drove off to the airport with a happy and warm feeling in my heart.

One of my friends and close clients called today to tell me an amazing story. Her fifteen-year-old son had to have part of his leg amputated as a result of cancer. There came a day in her life when the medical bills became so overwhelming that she realized she would have to face her creditors. After many hours of praying, interspersed with her duties taking care of her son, she began to telephone the creditors. But each of them told her that she did not owe them anything. It seems that, between some of her son's doctors and her insurance company, all her expenses had been taken care of. My friend has always had an unbelievable faith in things working out no matter what, and this incident confirmed that belief, for her and for me.

My Thoughts—

"Whatever you ask for in prayer with faith, you will receive."

—Matthew 21:22

Around ten percent of the individuals I train make significant changes in their lives as a result of my training. Among many traits these people exhibit, one stands out above all others: their faith. They know without a doubt that what they desire in life will become manifest. They are patient and joyful, strong in the inner knowledge that their desires and prayers are being answered, even if they cannot always recognize that process.

My Thoughts—

"For we walk by faith, not by sight."

—II Corinthians 5:7

When I am in need of something and it has not manifested in a way that I can see, I am challenged. When I become impatient or begin to doubt myself, I realize that I am failing to show faith in God. God comes to meet me, but meets me only as far in my consciousness as I have progressed. Either I believe in my spirit, or I do not. There is no gray area here. Closing the gap between my spirit and my humanity makes my desires manifest. It is the primary purpose of my life.

My Thoughts—

"Faith is believing what we do not see. The reward of this faith is to see what we believe."

—St. Augustine

There have been times in my life that my faith has been tested. Whether my challenge was with a relationship, my health, or my financial condition, things during these times looked extremely bleak to me. But as a result of these challenges, I realized was that I was out of connection with my divinity. I know that, in any situation, I cannot possibly lose faith if I truly am connected to my spirit. How can I stay in connection with God in my good moments as well in times of challenge?

My Thoughts—

"Now, faith is the substance of things hoped for, the evidence of things not seen."

—Hebrews 11:1

Until I consciously achieve union with my divinity and learn how to sustain my connection with it, I need to remember to *tell God what I desire.* I am never alone; God is within me, and I must remember that everything in my life is designed to teach me what I should do to maintain this connection. My faith is strengthened because I know, without a doubt, that everything I desire is already at hand. Even though there are many moments when I allow myself to react to things in an inappropriate way, I remember my challenges are opportunities for growth. Life is such a wonderful and unfolding adventure.

My Thoughts—

"Remember—when life's path is steep, keep your mind even."

—Horace

The crux of my relationship with faith is learning to discriminate between what is visible and invisible in my life. I have been programmed to equate my existence by what I visibly manifest in my life—possessions, achievements. My faith dares me to go beyond what my human eyes can see to manifestations of the spirit. I realize that I am developing my true eyes—my spiritual eyes—which are able to see God's hand at work in both the visible and invisible world. What examples can I think of which illustrate this realization?

My Thoughts—

"I believe; help my unbelief."

—Mark 9:24

I surrender to God's will in situations that cannot be readily understood. I have faith that I am part of a wonderful unfolding mystery. I see Spirit's wisdom in each moment of my life, even in times of adversity. My spiritual growth often comes in unexpected ways and always provides me with an opportunity to grow. In what situations have I practiced my faith in a positive way?

My Thoughts—

"Faith consists in believing when it is beyond the power of reason to believe. It is not enough that a thing be possible for it to be believed."

—Voltaire

In seeking manifestation of what I desire, my only task is to know what I desire, feel it strongly and express it. The three most powerful words I know after I have turned over my desires and problems to Spirit are: *It is done!* Once I have turned my desires over to Spirit, my work is done. I give no other thought or concern to the situation.

My Thoughts—

"How soon will you realize that the only thing you don't have is the direct experience that there is nothing you need that you don't have?"

—Ken Keyes

How do I know if I am in a state of faith? I know by my feeling of peace. No worry. No anxiety. My mind sometimes wants to interfere with this peaceful process, but I gently turn my attention to that inner place of peace. It is here that I reside with my higher self—my divinity.

My Thoughts—

"Be faithful to that which exists within yourself."

—Andre Gide

Today, my wife and I were discussing how much anxiety is being created in the world over the possibility of war with Iraq, the conflict between Israel and the Palestinians, and terrorism. I feel that anxiety at times, but my faith tells me that consciousness is unfolding. I try to see these events through my spiritual eyes. I know that one day we will be in peace on this planet. It is the only choice. It is my choice. It is part of our divine inheritance.

My Thoughts—

"We do not see things as they are—we see things as we are."

—Author Unknown

Today, I realized what surrender is all about. When I turn a problem or challenge over to Spirit, I am doing so in faith—from a place of knowing that everything is in divine order. Faith is one of the bridges between my divinity and my humanity.

My Thoughts—

"Instead of asking God to fix our bank accounts and body or bring a soul mate to our door, we should ask and meditate for a healing of consciousness . . . Then we accept the healing, and turn everything over to the Presence within."

—*The Jesus Code*, John Randolph Price

CHAPTER 9

GRATITUDE

"Everything that God, the source and substance of all, creates in this world flows naturally from the essence of God's divine nature. Creation is not a choice but a necessity. It is God's nature to unfold time and space."

—Avot 6:2 (Judaism)

I t always intrigues me to meet individuals whose divine presence shows in their eyes, and in the way they express and carry themselves. I want to relate a story about such a gentleman—for the purposes of this story, I'll call him "Sam."

In my own work, I offer workshops and retreats for the companies with whom I work. I was conducting a workshop for a school district in 1996 and had scheduled it at a spiritual retreat center that Sam and his wife run in South Texas. When I pulled into the parking lot of the retreat center, Sam drove up to my car in a golf cart to help me unload my supplies. As I went to shake his hand, I noticed right away that his face and his demeanor conveyed a sense of peace. His eyes were bright and shiny, and he spoke to me in a very caring way.

At first, we made small talk; I mentioned to him that the weather appeared to be cooperating for the retreat, and that would ensure a successful retreat for everyone. He looked at me and said that, regardless of weather or other circumstances, every day was a blessing to him. Curious as to what was inspiring this attitude in him, I asked him about his life and how he came to the spiritual renewal center.

Sam told me a bit about his life, and said that a year ago he had suffered a serious heart attack. He had been transported by ambulance to the hospital and when he arrived there, his heart had stopped beating. The doctors had worked feverishly to revive him. He told me that he left his body and that he watched the doctors working on him. I knew, from other accounts I had read, that Sam was describing a "near death" experience to me.

In these accounts, it is a common theme that those who die momentarily leave their bodies and continue to witness events occurring in the room. Sam told me that when he was out of his body he was drawn to a bright light. The love that he felt was unbelievable. There were people there, and though he could not recognize them, they told him that his work was not over yet, and that he was loved and protected. Within a few moments, to the surprise of the doctors around him, Sam woke up on the surgical table. He immediately asked for his wife.

In intensive care, he recounted to her the entire story of being out of his body, meeting his spiritual helpers, and what he was told. "From that day forward," he told me, "I have been in awe of each moment of life. Every second of life has been precious to me." He said that, in those moments in the light, he had felt a love that he could not describe in words, and that the overwhelming feeling he had was one of *gratitude*. He explained to me that for the first time in his life, he really knew what gratitude was about. Now, whether Sam is cleaning the toilet or holding hands with his wife, his love for God has been truly transformed and reinforced by his near-death experience.

~ ~ ~ ~ ~ ~ ~ ~ ~

As you may know, there are many books written by individuals who have had near-death experiences. What they recount is amazingly similar to the story Sam told me; for all of them, the message is that death is not the final stage, and we are surrounded by many spiritual helpers.

I have met many individuals who have had near-death experiences, and in addition to a similarity in their experience, they also share a positive and uplifting attitude about life. They are thankful for every little thing and every moment in their lives. The good news is that you do not have to have a near-death experience to achieve this state of joy and gratitude. You only have to decide, today, whether you wish to embrace life with passion, love, intention, and of course, gratitude. Once you have truly embraced a mindset of gratitude all of the time, then the choices you make in life will be reflected from this state of mind and heart.

My wife, Susan, inspires me. She is so loving and caring toward me and all people in her life. In 1998, I asked God to bring me my soul mate. I made this request with deep emotion and conviction. About a year later, I met Susan at a workshop, and we fell in love at first sight. I am so grateful to Spirit for having brought such a wonderful soul into my life. Who else has Spirit brought into my life that I am grateful for each day?

My Thoughts—

"I can no other answer make but thanks, and thanks, and ever thanks."

—William Shakespeare

I have had many wonderful teachers, but one had a particularly profound effect on my life. He was my high school foreign language teacher. He saw something in me at a time when I was very insecure and had no confidence. I traveled with him and some of my classmates to Europe one summer and the Orient in another summer. He believed in me, and provided me with life experiences that I will always be grateful for. Who else has Spirit put into my life who has helped me along my path?

My Thoughts—

"Gratitude is the heart's memory."

—Anonymous

My son continues to be one of my best teachers. He has taught me about integrity. As often happens with young people, there was a time when my son was asked to do something questionable that the rest of his friends were doing. When he told me about this situation, I asked him why he did not go along with his friends. He said that it would not have been the honest thing to do. He made me think about where I could be more honest in my life. Thank you, Ben.

My Thoughts—

"Gratitude is the sign of noble souls."

—*Androcles,* Aesop

I sometimes have trouble finding words to thank God and all my spiritual helpers, visible and invisible, for working with me in this lifetime. They have been so patient with me. When I want to gauge the spiritual progress I am making in life, I look around me. I am so blessed to have such wonderful people surrounding me. My heart is filled with such gratitude for life. The best is yet to come!

My Thoughts—

"Got no check books, got no banks—still I'd like to express my thanks—I got the sun in the mornin' and the moon at night."

—Irving Berlin

I admire my daughter's value system. Though she would never acknowledge or understand that she has an articulated value system, I am amazed at the choices she makes. Many times her decisions are contrary to what her friends are urging her to do. My daughter reminds me of the importance of speaking my truth without worrying how people might take it. Thank you, Amanda.

My Thoughts—

"Within this wall of flesh, there is a soul counts thee her creditor."

—*King John*, Act III, Sc. 3, 1.20, William Shakespeare

I have spent much time delineating and retracing my life story in order to recognize the high points and examine what I can learn from the low points. In looking at my life, I see I have attracted some individuals whom I have allowed to cause me some discomfort. I need to remember that these are divine beings and some were really my greatest teachers in disguise. I have come to appreciate the lessons they have taught me.

My Thoughts—

"Some people complain because God put thorns on roses,
while others praise him for putting roses among thorns."

—Anonymous

I like to keep a gratitude journal where I can write about what I am grateful for each day. I believe learning to be consciously grateful in each moment is one way to maintain connection with my divinity. I truly feel the divine presence when I am practicing gratitude.

My Thoughts—

"Every day's a gift. Treat it kindly. Share it with joy."

—Author Unknown

I am filled with thanks for the opportunity to be alive. I am centered in truth and peace as I accept the many blessings that I receive constantly.

My Thoughts—

"One should count each day as a separate life."

—Seneca

Recently, both of my parents passed away. I was blessed to have made the time to tell them, before they passed on, how grateful I was for them and for all that they had provided for me. I saw a man today whose father had just passed away. He was filled with so much bitterness toward his father that he was actually relieved that his father had passed away. I gently reminded him that he and I were here because of our parents. I helped him understand that, even though his father was no longer in this world, he could still make peace with his father through forgiveness.

My Thoughts—

"Thou hast given so much to me . . . Give one thing more— a grateful heart."

—George Herbert

My dogs bring me a sense of constant joy, and nothing makes me happier than to spend the entire day with them. They are such unconditional spirits who put up with me in my highs as well as my lows. I told them that. In the middle of sharing my thoughts with them, they began barking at me. They wanted a treat. I still told them I was grateful to them. They appeared to be grateful for the treat. It is human to look at our lives and recognize what inspires us in our own lives to be grateful; but it is useful to remember the lessons of my dogs, who are grateful in each and every present moment.

My Thoughts—

"He that urges gratitude pleads the cause both of God and men, for without it we can neither be sociable nor religious."

—Seneca

I express my gratitude in a conscious effort to acknowledge the presence of a higher power in my life. When I am blessing my yard, or my animals, or someone in my life, I am reminding myself that God exists in all forms of life. Expressing gratitude is a way for me to avoid taking life for granted. Each moment is a blessing.

My Thoughts—

"May silent thanks at least to God be given with a full heart; our thoughts are heard in heaven."

—William Wordsworth

Today, I received a letter from one of my clients. It expressed how grateful he was for my help. I was caught off guard by the letter because I had no idea I had that much impact on him, or that he felt such gratitude toward me. I thanked him for his kind thoughts, and I gently reminded myself that my work has a positive effect in ways I may not even know.

My Thoughts—

"Gratitude is not only the memory but the homage of the heart—rendered to God for his goodness."

—Nathaniel Parker Willis

Today, I held a door into a store open for an elderly lady, and she turned to thank me. She said that often, people walk on out the door and let it close on her. I told her thanks for reminding me to pay attention. I enjoy opening *doors* for people; I enjoy being a source of gratitude in their lives!

My Thoughts—

"From David learn to give thanks for everything. Every furrow in the Book of Psalms is sown with the seeds of thanksgiving."

—Jeremy Taylor

CHAPTER 10

LOVE

"And God said to the soul: I desired you before the world began. I desire you now as you desire me. And where the desires of two come together, there love is perfected."

—Mechthild of Magdeburg (Christianity)

I n his many journeys, the Buddha met a man one day who appeared to be upset over his teachings. The individual scolded the Buddha and chastised him while the Buddha just stood there politely listening in silence.

When the man had ended his tirade, the Buddha respectfully asked, "My brother, have you finished?" The man replied sarcastically, "I have finished, but I am not your brother."

The Buddha's eyes filled with love and he answered, "We are all brothers, you and I. If you were to offer a gift and it was not accepted, who would remain the recipient of the gift?"

Now the man had to think about that and he finally answered, "The giver of the gift."

"My brother, you have spoken well," the Buddha replied. The Buddha continued by saying, "All of that condemnation you offered me, in love I refuse to accept. Therefore, you, the creator of this gift, are also the recipient and it remains with you. Only through love can you return it to its source of nothingness."

~ ~ ~ ~ ~ ~ ~ ~ ~

This story was a reminder of something I heard recently. I was attending a workshop with my wife, Susan, and the presenter asked a very simple question: "What is love?" As I listened to the responses of the workshop participants, I heard many insightful interpretations on this subject. In my own mind, I was constructing my intellectual response to this query.

Yet, as the last person answered the question, we all realized that there were no adequate words to describe this subject. Love just is! We know how it feels, but it is a hard word to define.

Thousands of books have been written on this subject, and many movies have been made about love. I have come to the conclusion, though, that love can really only be defined by how it manifests.

For example, I can enjoy the beauty of a flower garden or the exquisite landscape of a redwood forest. Perhaps the beauty of a crystal or two playful bear cubs playing with one another can invoke a feeling inside me. Words can never adequately convey the love in these moments; only by experiencing love's manifestations can we understand its power.

Ultimately, love for me is truly defined by certain people in my life. My wife is pure love to me. She is a very kind, compassionate and giving individual whose spirit touches everyone she encounters in a loving way. The love I feel for my children, Ben and Amanda, remind me on a daily basis of the power and feeling of love.

As I think about how love feels, I realize that it is really Spirit that I love, and when love manifests, it manifests as Spirit. Spirit is manifesting in my life each day through many forms and individuals, and what I am experiencing when I experience "love" is really that divine connection.

My final thoughts to you on this subject are to suggest that I have found a clue as to why creation and Spirit need love. Spirit does not have a way to manifest itself without love. It needs some form of substance to give itself identity. The Divine needs us in order to know itself.

Love is the connection that bridges the gap between the visible and invisible world. Just as a tea bag needs water in order to become tea, the Divine needs us to be able to express Its loving presence.

Remember that where love exists, there can be no darkness. When we express love through our words and actions, there can be no hate. Love is the essence of all things visible in the Universe. When we can embrace and accept this fact, then heaven on earth will have become manifest, and there will be peace on this planet.

As a parent, I do not own my kids. All I can do is direct them when I feel it is necessary, and let them learn from the choices they make. My unconditional love commits me to loving them no matter what. I believe that the Divine operates the same way. I am given the power to choose and the gift of experiencing the results of the choices I've made, no matter what the consequences. Regardless, the Divine will always be with me to welcome me in my happiness and in my sorrow.

My Thoughts—

"Love teaches even asses to dance."

—French Proverb

When I am feeling love in my heart, this sensation is simultaneously being transmitted to my brain and every cell in my body. At the same time, this intense feeling is being sent out into my outer world and by law, the only thing that can return is love. Sometimes, it returns in lessons I find difficult to recognize, such as clients who do not seem to appreciate what I am teaching them. I sometimes find my love conditional in these circumstances, but I know divine love knows no limits.

My Thoughts—

"A man cannot be comfortable without his own approval."

—Mark Twain

On the physical level, the organ that keeps me alive is the heart. The heart is also the source of my emotions and feelings. I can transform any negative energy by concentrating on and feeling positive and loving memories. I believe the heart is the gateway to my divinity, and love keeps that connection open.

My Thoughts—

"He who loves the world as his body may be entrusted with the empire."

—Tao Te Ching

I forgive myself for the choices I have made in the past that have caused pain to me or to someone else. I must remember that I was making the best choices I could at the time, based on where I was in consciousness and in my own growth. Forgiveness is about self-love; forgiveness allows my divinity to come forth. Forgiving myself allows me to feel divine love, and to recognize my mistakes as the path of divine growth.

My Thoughts—

"Can there be a love which does not make demands on its objects?"

—Confucius

When God gave me the power of choice, that act was, in itself, a pure act of love. God's gift of choice can result in my making mistakes, but I know those mistakes are part of my growth. Whether I choose to perceive my struggles as the wisdom of God at work, or whether I choose to blame others for my struggles, choice remains God's gift to me, and God hopes only for my happiness and well-being. For example, I need to free myself of any idea that God wants me to sacrifice myself or live in poverty. God's love is abundance in its totality.

My Thoughts—

"Love is, above all, the gift of oneself."

—John Anouilh

Once, someone at a presentation asked me whether I believed evil exists. My answer was, "Yes." Each time I hold back any love or caring from someone, I feed the energy of evil. Every time I am critical or judgmental toward someone, I help evil to grow. If I spell evil backwards, I arrive at the word "live." How am I choosing to live my life?

My Thoughts—

"We must love one another or die."

—W.H. Auden

How can I learn to become a more loving person? Just by allowing myself to fall in love. In each moment, I allow myself to fall in love. Whether I feel joy or despair, I choose to engage life from the perceptive of how Spirit would handle the situation. Just as I can jump into a swimming pool and be totally immersed in water, imagine the entire Universe as a huge swimming pool of Spirit. I am immersed in the love of Spirit.

My Thoughts—

"The universe is but one great city, full of beloved ones, divine and human by nature, endeared to each other."

—Epictetus

I realized one day how many talented and loving people are a part of my life. This realization was even more powerful when I remembered that the individuals who bless my life are a reflection of me. I attracted them into my life. If I perceive these individuals as being talented and loving, then I must also be this way. I cannot see in another that which is not conscious in myself. What qualities do those I love affirm in me?

My Thoughts—

"All, everything that I understand, I understand only because I love."

—*War and Peace*, Leo Tolstoy

I do not want any regrets in my life. Let me make a promise to myself from this day forward to seek divine love in *all* of life, no matter how a situation is presented to me. I choose to live from this divine space instead of in fear and envy. What situations challenge me to see in terms of love, and how can I work to do so? In what situations do I put love into practice well?

My Thoughts—

Let all that you do be done in love."

—I Corinthians 16:14

I open wide the door to my heart, and I let the love flow out to all of life. I express my feelings, and I do so without worrying how I might appear to someone else. I choose to allow God's love to embrace me, guide me, and support me. I extend this invitation to my higher self as I create a bridge between my humanity and my divinity. Love is my building block for this bridge.

My Thoughts—

"What will survive all of us is love."

—Phillip Larkin

I love myself. This is truly the only relationship! Who am I loving when I love myself?

My Thoughts—

"Who falls for love of God shall rise a star."

—Ben Jonson

I once heard a motivational speaker talk about love and fear. He used the analogy of how fear knocked on the door, love answered, and no one was there. Where there is love, fear and evil cannot exist.

My Thoughts—

"A man whose eyes love opens risks his soul—his dancing breaks beyond the mind's control."

—Farid Ud-Din Attar

The single most powerful affirmation I have been exposed to on the subject of love is the following: "I send out the Christ Energy before me to heal and harmonize all conditions in my life." When this affirmation is said with great emotion and intent, I establish what I wish to happen this day, and always, just by affirming Christ's loving presence in my life.

My Thoughts—

"Love conquers all: and let us too surrender to love."

—Virgil

One of the purest acts of love I have seen was my wife, who is a school principal, helping out a homeless family who was living in their station wagon with no clothes or food. This family sent their children to my wife's school. My wife took them to a local department store to buy clothes and paid for a couple of nights in a warm room at a local hotel. The family was very thankful for my wife's kindness.

My Thoughts—

"Love is all we have, the only way that each can help the other."

—Euripides

Science has proven through magnetic resonance imaging that a certain part of the brain lights up when a person in a state of joy and love. The brain produces positive chemicals when we are in these heightened states. Love is my true natural state, and I can exhibit it in my work, in my relationships, and in my thoughts and feelings. What areas of my life can I rely on love to transform?

My Thoughts—

"Love's conqueror is he whom love conquers."

—*The Walled Garden of Truth: The Hadiqa*, Hakim Sanai

AUTHOR'S NOTE

*R**emembering Our Spirit* is the first volume in the *Practical Spirituality* series. I have several more books planned in this series, and I'd like to hear from you. If you have any stories about your own spiritual discoveries or adventures, or any thoughts that you would like to share with me, please send them to me at the address below. If you do *not* wish me to include your story in my future books, please note that in your letter. Otherwise, I might include your stories or thoughts in my future volumes, without using your name. Thank you; I wish you much success and happiness in your life.

David D. Dameron
PO Box 5911
San Antonio, TX 78201

website: *www.daviddameron.com*

BVG